2002

CLEMENTINE HUNTER

American Folk Artist

A woman with great natural dignity, strong opinions about what is right, a well-defined sense of self worth, a disinclination to suffer fools gladly, and, above all, a droll sense of humor that is at once earthy and whimsical.

ROBERT AND YVONNE RYAN

Clementine Hunter (c. 1945). Photo from the Mildred Bailey Collection, Natchitoches, Louisiana.

CLEMENTINE HUNTER
American Folk Artist

By James L. Wilson

Pelican Publishing Company
GRETNA 1990

First printing, November 1988
Second printing, June 1990

Library of Congress Cataloging-in-Publication Data

Wilson, James L. (James Lynwood)
    Clementine Hunter, American folk artist / James L. Wilson.
        p.   cm.
    Bibliography: p.
    Includes index.
    ISBN 0-88289-658-X
    1. Hunter, Clementine.   2. Afro-American painting—Louisiana—
Natchitoches.   3. Primitivism in art—Louisiana—Natchitoches.   4. Painting,
Modern—20th century—Louisiana—Natchitoches.
I. Title.
ND237.H915A4 1988
759.13—dc19   88-2068
                                                                CIP

Photos of Clementine Hunter's art in this volume were taken by John C.
Guillet, except for those on the following pages: Paul Rico: pp. 51, 52, 53,
54, 55, 58, 84, 85, 86, 92 (Uncle Tom), 95, 96, 97; W. I. Bell: pp. 114, 125;
B. A. Cohen: p. 83

Manufactured in Hong Kong

Published by Pelican Publishing Company, Inc.
1101 Monroe Street, Gretna, Louisiana 70053

Contents

Clementine Hunter in front of her house near Melrose Plantation (c. 1950). Photo from the Melrose Collection, Cammie G. Henry Research Center, Eugene P. Watson Library, Northwestern State University, Natchitoches, Louisiana.

Foreword

In late summer, 1963, I returned from graduate study to my home in Natchitoches, Louisiana—the place of my birth. Soon after, I made my way down Cane River to Clementine Hunter's house to buy one of her paintings. The occasion profoundly affected my life.

I will start at the beginning. In 1946, a few of Clementine Hunter's oil paintings were sent to Natchitoches by her friend, François Mignon, to be displayed and offered for sale at Millspaugh's Drug Store on Front Street. I frequently visited the drug store and there first saw her work. I remember how "Miss Toosie" Millspaugh and I shared our amusement at the scenes of plantation life that included childlike figures of black people at work and at play. Certainly, we did not consider the paintings to be of value in any way historically, aesthetically, or culturally. After all, they had been painted by an illiterate black servant who lived most of her life on a plantation. And although the price of a painting was only a dollar or so, I never considered buying one.

But neither could I forget those paintings. And through the years, as Clementine Hunter continued to work at her art, I came to realize that something in me had responded to those paintings in Millspaugh's Drug Store.

Eventually, I went to visit the artist at her home on Melrose Plantation. As I approached her small, unpainted, wood frame house that summer day in 1963, I saw a sign by the front door that announced to all who read it, "Clementine Hunter, Artist, 25 cents to Look."

Clementine answered my knock at the door and rather grudgingly, it seemed to me, brought out several of her oil paintings that were for sale. She appeared indifferent to the possibility of a sale and was not at all interested in conversation.

I selected the picture that I found most interesting and appealing, a black Jesus on the cross at Calvary. I paid her three dollars and left.

After the black Jesus was framed, I hung it in a place of prominence in my home. Although I had intended to buy only one painting, I soon realized that it was speaking to me in a compelling way. After a few months, I returned to the artist's house and this time bought a wonderful painting of six black women in red hats picking cotton in the field. Sometime later I bought a wedding scene. As others followed, I realized I had fallen completely in love with Clementine Hunter's work.

Year by year, painting by painting, the artist touched my life.

She and I eventually became friends, but it took time. She was a very reserved person with a regal demeanor, who enjoyed her privacy. (I often envisioned her as a tribal queen enthroned somewhere in ancient, faraway Africa. She would have ruled with great dignity and wonderfully well.) In time, the artist chose to recognize me and call me by name. She told François Mignon that I was "just like home folks," and after that I was often referred to by him as that—"home folks." As for my feelings for her, I came to respect, admire, and love her. I do not like to consider what my life would have been if I had not bought the painting of the black Jesus that summer day in 1963. Much of the best part of my life has been amazingly influenced by Clementine Hunter.

Not only has my life been enriched by knowing Clementine, and by living with her paintings in my home, but she also was the reason that my life and Mignon's life came together and touched in a very special way. Without François, there doubtless would have been no Clementine Hunter, the artist. Although she might have been creative in many ways, she would not have received the great recognition she did without François's support.

He encouraged her, supplied her with oil paints and materials, and, most of all, promoted her through his writing and his influential friends.

Clementine and I often talked about past times on Melrose Plantation, and she spoke fondly of "Mister François." I am not sure that she realized how much he influenced her life, but I know that she loved him.

I live in a house that I bought because of Clementine Hunter. After fifteen years of steadily collecting her work, I had no wall space left in my small house to display her paintings. On July 4, 1978, I moved into Chaplin House—a large Victorian house built in 1892 and listed on the National Register of Historic Places. I carefully restored the house so that it could serve as a place to display Clementine Hunter's works.

Chaplin House is now visited by hundreds of people annually for the purpose of viewing her paintings. All sorts of people visit—most simply to enjoy the paintings, but others come as students or critics. Writers and photographers from newspapers and magazines visit, as do national radio and television people accompanied by well-known personalities.

Why all of this interest in a tiny black woman who could neither read nor write and who spent all of her life in rural northwest Louisiana—a person who could have lived and died in obscurity, as did countless others of her race, place, and time? What do all of these people write and say and feel and believe about the late Clementine Hunter and her work? Was she a great artist? Was she an important historian? There is disagreement over these questions.

All agree that she was among the best-known folk artists in America. No longer is that questioned—her place is secure; any art historian familiar with folk art will affirm that. But not to be forgotten—and possibly most important of all—is Clementine

Hunter's contribution in passing on the memory of a culture now gone.

She has recorded, for all generations to come (and most importantly, from the perspective of a participant), life on a Southern plantation during the first half of the twentieth century. She was one of those women picking cotton and wearing a red hat to shade her from the hot summer sun. She was one of those women who boiled clothes in the black iron pot for the plantation owner. She was there on Saturday night at the honky-tonk, down the road from the plantation. And she was there on Sunday morning when the plantation folk were baptized in Cane River. This colorful, unique, joyous life that has passed from the American scene was the life she lived and the life she recorded, in the only way she knew—with oil and brush and canvas.

Yes, Clementine Hunter was a great folk artist. And, yes, she was an important cultural historian. But did she care? Not a whit. She would quickly say that she could not take credit for her work. "God puts those pictures in my head and I just puts them on the canvas, like he wants me to," she often said.

And so, it is my pleasure to introduce this book to you—a book that accurately and sensitively records the personality, life, and work of a most unlikely gift from God to the world, Clementine Hunter. As you read, let the spirit of her and her art touch your spirit. You will be richly rewarded.

MILDRED HART BAILEY
Natchitoches, Louisiana

Clementine Hunter and Mildred Bailey in front of the African House, Melrose Plantation, 1978. Photo by John C. Guillet.

François Mignon (c. 1955). Photo from the Mignon Collection, Cammie G. Henry Research Center, Eugene P. Watson Library, Northwestern State University, Natchitoches, Louisiana.

Acknowledgments

This book has greatly benefited from the help of others and I would like to identify and thank them here.

The project would have been extremely difficult without the patient and unending help of Dr. Mildred Hart Bailey. She provided voluminous research material as well as constant counseling, guidance, and yes, even inspiration. Likewise for Thomas N. Whitehead, who provided anecdotal insights, answered numerous questions, and willingly reviewed every aspect of the book. Ann Williams Brittain, too, was helpful and supportive throughout the endeavor.

For assistance in the research of key details, I would like to thank Genevieve Tobin, Father John Cunningham, Jerry Brungart, Eugene Lavespere, Carol Wells, and Mildred Lee.

For her patient reading of the manuscript, and her sharp eye for detail, thanks go to Elva Torgrimson. For their daily kindness and enthusiasm, I thank Ben Rushing, Sr., Bena Rushing, and Ben Rushing, Jr.

I would like to give a special word of thanks to my mother, Lee Cummings, whose help in transcribing tapes and preparing the final manuscript made the entire task pleasant . . . and on time.

And finally, I would like to thank my wife, Mar'Sue, for taking up the slack when it was necessary, and for bearing with me throughout the writing of this book.

This book is dedicated, with love, to the children: Allison, Rachele, Nicole, and Geoffrey.

JAMES L. WILSON
Natchitoches, Louisiana

Clementine Hunter and Mildred Bailey, Ann Brittain, Jack Brittain, and Thomas Whitehead at her 98th birthday party, 1985.

CLEMENTINE HUNTER
American Folk Artist

Clementine Hunter. From the Mildred Bailey Collection, Natchitoches, Louisiana.

BIOGRAPHY

Introduction

IT IS SPRING, 1987. The home in which Clementine Hunter lives and paints, in her one-hundredth year, is a small trailer house in a modest rural neighborhood some fifteen miles south of Natchitoches, Louisiana. The trailer house is white with peeling paint, fronted by a frazzled screen porch. It sits amid several country blocks of similarly small, dingy trailers with an occasional simple white A-frame. The roads in the neighborhood are packed gravel with slumping shoulders. The road leading from the neighborhood out to the main highway, which winds along Cane River into town, is better; it is blacktop.

Inside the home the furnishings are spare. The light is dim. Save for a few amenities such as air conditioning, carpeted floors, and a color television set, there is not much difference between this home and the several plantation shanties she was born in, grew up in, worked in, and raised her family in. Except that she owns this home.

Hunter still accepts visitors this spring, and there are many who call on her: friends, fans, journalists, social and cultural historians fueling dissertations, and art collectors. Most find her at home, not so much because she is enfeebled by her arthritis and the halting infirmities that time has forced upon her, but because home has been and always will be the central place in her life. Not in one hundred years has she been over a hundred miles from home. She is invariably neatly dressed, perhaps in a dark green dress with small white patterns and a lacy collar. Her clothes are nicely ironed. She has on a wig of loose black ringlets that curl down to big rhinestone earrings. She may be wearing her pair of wing-frame glasses.

Usually she greets a visitor from her seat in a big, lumpy living room chair that has been covered with a bright red throw. Her disposition is generally even, though she has been known to be mischievously impolite—once she poked her head out the window and told some earnest person looking for the famous Clementine Hunter that the old woman lived down the road.

Her thin legs are crossed gingerly. In front of her is an ever-present aluminum walker, a rosary looped over one handle. On the floor sits a cup where she spits snuff. Her eyes are bright and searching. When she smiles, she does so wryly, with a slight tuck in one corner of her mouth, and flashes bright white teeth highlighted with gold caps.

She is pretty today. Is she going somewhere? Nowhere at all. But she dresses up every day, a form of adherence, possibly, to the plantation custom of being ready at all times for the coming of the Lord, with burial clothes neatly pressed and set aside. The darkly paneled living room walls of the trailer are lined with certificates of honor and award. There is a framed letter from President Ronald Reagan, another from U.S. Senator J. Bennett Johnston. There is a proclamation from Edwin Edwards, governor of Louisiana in 1987, making her an honorary colonel and aide-de-camp. There is an honorary Doctor of Fine Arts degree from Northwestern State University of Louisiana.

The centerpiece on the main wall is a gilt-framed, plaster bas-relief of the Last Supper. Elsewhere are photographs of family—children, grandchildren, and great-grandchildren—and friends. Some are black friends, some are white. Nowhere in the room are there any paintings by the now-famous black American artist Clementine Hunter.

Off the living room is a narrow hall which leads, first, to a tiny bedroom occupied almost entirely with a single bed and a low, three-drawer chest. The iron-framed bed is overseen by a large crucifix. It is where the artist sleeps a few hours each night.

Midway down the hall, the smells of linseed oil, turpentine, and oil paints take over. The "paintin' room" is beyond the closed door at the end.

It is unexpectedly bright inside Hunter's studio. The room is small, no more than twelve feet square, and paneled with that same dusky veneer found throughout the house. But in this room there are windows on three sides, each draped with a lacey sheer curtain that allows sunlight to pour in. In the center of the room is a knee-high table overlaid with a three-foot square slab of half-inch plywood. The plywood serves as a worktable. It is clustered with murky jars of turpentine sprouting dozens of paint-spattered artist brushes. Around the jars lie countless crumpled tubes of Grumbacher, staunched with patches of tissue as if they were a band of rag-tag soldiers fallen in service to the queen. The entire perimeter of the plywood serves as the artist's palette. Vivid colors—yellows, reds, blues, blacks, greens—surround the board in glistening mounds of paint often an inch thick. A few of the colors are lightly streaked (signs of mixing and dabbing and stirring), but Hunter's penchant for the untainted primaries is evident. Dominating the board is a mound of bright yellow paint, hollowed like a volcano by a brush that favors its warm, healing glow.

Apart from the small straightbacked chair which sits beside the artist's worktable, there is little else in the room. There are a few blank canvas boards in varying sizes tossed off in a pile in one corner of the room. Leaning against the wall is a newly "marked" Hunter canvas, a pencilled rough frame-up of a picture that she says "just came into my mind." If there are any Hunter originals in the house, they are in a makeshift gallery adjacent to the studio. The room, which doubles as a guest bedroom for grand-children and great-grandchildren, is fitted with another small single bed and dresser. Typically, the gallery will have a few pictures set up to dry, either commissioned work or, like the pencilled canvas in the studio, works that were inspired, "put into my mind by God." The paintings—perhaps a *Cotton Picking*, a

François Mignon and Clementine Hunter study a series of early Hunter works (c. 1945). Photo from the Mignon Collection, Cammie G. Henry Research Center, Eugene P. Watson Library, Northwestern State University, Natchitoches, Louisiana.

Washday, a *Watermelon,* a *Big House,* a *Zinnias Looking at You*—sit on the bed propped against the wall. If more room is needed, they go on the floor.

It is not often this spring that a visitor will find Hunter at work on a painting. Her age and infirmities have also cooled her artistic fires.

But whenever she is moved to work, then work she must. Slowly she will hoist herself out of the living room chair and into the frame of her walker. Her frail, diminutive body follows the walker, step by cautious step, down the narrow hall. She moves deliberately, testing each new step before she takes it. When she arrives at the chair in her studio, she tests its stability with her fingertip, delicately pressing the center of the cushion like a cat pawing a tenuous ledge. Convinced she is safe, she slowly turns and sits.

She seems transformed the moment she sits down beside her palette. Her back straightens and she immediately seems more responsive, almost perky. Suddenly she has no fear, and her calm, analytical eyes begin to assess her environment. Meanwhile her mind begins to race ahead.

Soon she turns to the worktable and begins to finger a brush. First one, then another—slowly, very slowly. She studies each one carefully, rolling it between her fingertips as if counting all the hairs. She becomes fascinated by each brush. A faint smile comes to her face. She remembers, now, that she must clean the brush.

As she does, her mind moves further ahead; her eyes look around the room. There is light, there is color, there is a canvas marked and ready.

She reaches for the canvas and pulls it across the floor into her lap. Her concentration becomes intense as she studies the coarse markings she had made sometime before. Soon they take on meaning to her. She turns to the colors on the plyboard, then to the brushes. In a moment, perhaps a very long moment, the brush is headed for a spot of color on the plyboard. And then it is moving toward the canvas.

The will to paint has had its way.

As she begins painting, her eyes begin to dance like the eyes of a child. The face of a one-hundred-year-old woman is gone. Colors fly. Some happy wonder is about to happen.

CHAPTER ONE

The Family

CLEMENTINE (PRONOUNCED "CLEMENTEEN") Hunter was born in late December of 1886 or early January of 1887 on Hidden Hill Plantation, a few miles south of Cloutierville, Louisiana. The plantation was a sprawling landscape of cotton fields and pecan groves bordered by rolling hills. It carried its name faithfully, sitting isolated from the flourishing mainstream of plantation life a little to the north. Hidden Hill had a reputation as a difficult place to live and work. Society was discouraged, pay was miserly, and while slavery was a thing of the past, the overseers were still often harsh—all bearing up the legend that the plantation had been the real-life inspiration for the novel *Uncle Tom's Cabin*. Hunter remembered it more simply; she called it a place "way down yonder at the end of the road. You don't see no birds, you don't see no nothin' down there where I was born."

She would not stay there long. Farm laborers followed the work, and her father, a hardworking field hand, saw his opportunity on the plantations to the north, in fabled Cane River Country. There, along the banks of the Cane River, was rich alluvial soil with bustling farm operations—not one but dozens and dozens of them. There were stores and churches and a school. And there, too, flowed a unique current of life—one that had been built by almost two centuries of heroic explorers and the legends and folkways of four disparate cultures: French, Spanish, American Indian, and African.

It was there by the Cane River (which would in time come to be known as "The Joyous Coast") that this family would soon begin to carve out a life.

Clementine was born to Antoinette Adams, who was unmarried at the time. Her father, Janvier (John) Reuben, was "a pure Frenchman," according to the artist. "All my people were Creoles. They say us Creoles got more different kinds of blood than any other people. When I was growing up all the folks on lower Cane River were Creoles . . . spoke nothing but French."

She knew her father's parents well. Her grandfather was "an old Irishman who traded horses up and down the road" during the Civil War. Her grandmother she described as a "little low lady with long black hair . . . a black Indian lady called 'MeMe' [may may]." Her maternal grandparents were Idole and Billy Zack Adams. The artist remembered her grandmother Idole as a slave brought to Louisiana from "Ol' Virginia" who lived to be 110 years old.

Janvier Reuben and Antoinette Adams were married on October 5, 1890, in the Catholic church of St. John the Baptist at Cloutierville. The couple had seven children: Clementine, Maria, Ida, Rosa, Edward, Simon, and John.

Clementine, who was the oldest, was also the smallest of the children. Her nickname was "TeBa" (tee bay), a shortened version of the French *petit bébé*, which means "little baby." (Her grandchildren and great-grandchildren upheld the tradition, calling her "Mama TeBa.") Clementine had said that she was originally named Clemence and that she changed her name to Clementine after she moved to Melrose Plantation years later. Census records of 1900 and 1910 show her as Clemence. Her baptismal record shows she was christened Clementiam, which, in Latin, would have been pronounced "Clemenciam."

It was when Hunter was still a young girl, perhaps five or six, that her father moved the family from Hidden Hill to Cloutierville. And it was soon after, at the Catholic school run by French-speaking nuns, that she got her first and only taste of formal education. She did not like it. The white children and the black children, despite being separated by a fence, were always somehow getting at one another. The nuns were very strict. And more to the point, Hunter just "never was much for school." She was a chronic runaway who did not stay in school long, as she recalled in one interview:

> . . . after about ten days I quit school. Didn't like it at all. So I never even learned any of the ABCs. And I have made out all right, too. All my life I have had a strong mother-wit, which is better than stuff you learn from books. Leastwise I can say I don't think I missed anything by not getting reading and writing. It's a heap of folks got book learning running out of their ears, but I can't say they is smart people.

Hunter was not pushed back into school because, as badly as her mother and father may have felt she needed it, they needed her more to work. "I was needed at home. Papa and Mama and my brothers and sisters all worked. We had to scuffle to keep things going."

Indeed, work was all the family knew, and so when the opportunity arose for yet more of it, they packed once again and headed north. As before, the move would take them only a few miles, geographically. But this move from Cloutierville to Melrose Plantation would be significant. Not only would it take the family finally into the plantation mainstream where work would be plentiful, but it would take a young Clementine, now fourteen or fifteen years of age, into what would become the heart and soul of her art.

CHAPTER TWO

The Melrose Influence

B Y THE TIME Janvier Reuben moved his family to Melrose Plantation it had long been established as the centerpiece of Cane River Country. Its beautiful Big House and attendant structures sat on the northwest bank of the Cane River, on grounds that stretched far to the east and west, along the river. In its glorious past it had included thousands of acres of cotton, corn, and tobacco, hundreds of head of cattle, and had required over two hundred slaves to maintain.

The history of Melrose began with Marie Thérèse Coincoin, a black slave born in 1742 into the household of Louis Juchereau de St. Denis, first commandant of the French post at Natchitoches. Coincoin was a woman of unusual energy, intelligence, and determination. She lived to be over seventy-three years old and was the matriarch of a family of fourteen children—four black and ten of Franco-African blood. Most remarkably, she had been able to gain her own freedom as well as the freedom of all of her children, and then build an agricultural empire second to none in the region. At the center of her holdings was the plantation she acquired in 1796 and called Yucca, after the profusion of yucca plants found on the grounds. It was the family's tribute to its own great spirit of determination and to the woman behind it all.

By the mid-1800s, however, victimized by their own bad management, the family lost the plantation. What followed was a wave of sales and seizures that would continue through Southern Reconstruction and would leave the house and grounds in serious disrepair. It was not until 1898, and the coming of another determined *grande dame*, that the plantation began to breathe life again.

It was in that year that John Hampton Henry and his wife, Carmelita ("Cammie") Garrett Henry, assumed ownership of the plantation and changed the name from Yucca to Melrose. "Miss

Cammie," as she was known to a wide circle of friends and acquaintances, was, like Coincoin, a woman of boundless energy and enthusiasm. She established early on her intentions of returning Melrose to its former condition.

She laid out an expansive plan for herself. There was a large family to be reared and an enormous household to maintain. There were gardens to be replanted and, in time, enlarged. There were colonial buildings to be saved from deterioration—buildings in which Coincoin and her sons and daughters had lived and flourished.

Too, there were matters of arts and letters. Miss Cammie was intent upon establishing an extensive Louisiana library at Melrose. She wanted to revive local arts and crafts. Above all, she wanted to restore the abiding sense of place, sense of history, that once belonged to the plantation.

Her ample dreams and desires are described in this excerpt from a 1973 publication by the Association for the Preservation of Historic Natchitoches:

> Local handicrafts which had almost been forgotten by other inhabitants of the region had to be revived; and the few remaining looms, long since fallen into disuse, had to be sought out and made serviceable for hand-weaving projects. Less fortunate neighbors of color had to be looked after. Cane River correspondence and journals of old days had to be sought out and the portraits and heirlooms of the colonial inhabitants had to be preserved. A collection of scrapbooks, the like of which had perhaps never before been initiated by any plantation mistress on such an extensive scale, had to be increased in material and intellectual scope. Time had to be found, too, for personal contacts with people living in different sections of the country who felt impelled to journey to Melrose to exchange ideas with Miss Cammie.

Melrose would in time become the mecca for arts, culture, and history that Miss Cammie envisioned. And during her fifty years as mistress she would welcome as guests to the great plantation many notables, including: Lyle Saxon, Harnett Kane, Alexander Woollcott, Roark Bradford, Rachel Field, Rose Franken, William Spratling, Gwen Bristow, Alberta Kinsey, Dr. Janet Miller, Arthur McArthur, Josiah Titzell, Ruth Cross Palmer, Edith Wyatt Moore, James Pipes Register, Ross Phares, Mary Land, William Brown Maloney, Ada Jack Carver, Carolyn Ramsey, Richard Avedon, Elemore Morgan, John C. Guillet, Caroline Dormon, and François Mignon.

But there were few more notable than would become the small, dark-skinned daughter of a field hand, who came to the place shortly after the turn of the century, and who would follow Marie Thérèse Coincoin and Cammie Garrett Henry as the third *femme extraordinaire* of Melrose Plantation.

Clementine Hunter's only remembrance of her family's move to Melrose was that it occurred when she was "not a little girl and not old enough to marry." She was, however, old enough to join her father in the field, and so she went immediately to work. Her father taught her to pick cotton. He could pick more than four hundred pounds a day, straddling one cotton row and snatching bolls from three rows in one circular swoop.

She spent many years in the cotton fields and preferred picking cotton to anything else on the plantation. But that did not mean she avoided other work. "I used to farm, hoe cotton, hoe corn, grow sugar cane, pick cotton—done all that," she said. There was season after season of pecan picking, for which she admitted a liking, although, "it was hard work; you had to stoop over a lot, you had to gather at least three hundred pounds or

Antoinette Adams Reuben, mother of Clementine Hunter. Photo from the Mildred Bailey Collection, Natchitoches, Louisiana.

Janvier Reuben, father of Clementine Hunter. Photo from the Mildred Bailey Collection, Natchitoches, Louisiana.

better a day to make it worthwhile." There were countless wash-days, there was firewood to be chopped, and there was her own family to start and to attend.

The father of Clementine's first two children was Charlie Dupree, a man fifteen years her senior. There is no record of her marriage to him, and she maintained they were never married, "just keepin' company." He was apparently extraordinary company, as described by one who knew the family well:

> Charlie Dupree, once familiarly known as Cuckoo Charlie, was an eccentric with a mechanical aptitude that appeared to be almost genius. He conceived and constructed a piano without ever having seen the instrument. From a description of a mechanical gadget he actually built a steam engine that would function.

Their first-born was a son, Joseph (Frenchie), born in 1907 near Melrose. A few years later they had a second child, Cora. Charlie Dupree died about 1914.

In January of 1924, Clementine married Emanuel Hunter, a woodchopper at Melrose Plantation. He was six years older than she, and, in her words, "a good Christian husband . . . he loved to work and he loved to have something . . . didn't want to never be without nothin'." They lived in worker's quarters on the plantation grounds.

The couple had five children, according to the artist: Agnes, King, Mary, and two who were stillborn and never named. Clementine was proud of the fact that she gave birth to seven children in all, "just like my mama did."

Her mother, Antoinette Reuben, died at Melrose Plantation in 1905. According to the artist, her mother died of dropsy, a colloquial reference to edema. Her father died at Melrose several years later.

Clementine continued to work in the fields throughout her childbearing years, most often in the cotton fields. "I picked cotton one morning just before I borned one of my babies. I remember how much it was—seventy-eight pounds. Then I went home, called the midwife, and borned my baby. It didn't worry me none. In a few days I was back in the fields," she recalled. With no hands to spare for baby-sitting duties, she would take her children with her to work, set them down at the turnrows, and check on them as she moved up and down the rows of cotton.

Clementine moved out of the fields and into full-time domestic duties at the plantation sometime in the late 1920s. Her new chores, as maid and occasional cook for the mistress of Melrose, included tending the vegetable gardens, doing laundry and ironing, and helping rear the Henry children.

It was here that she began to establish herself as a highly capable woman with a creative flair. She became known among the many guests of the plantation as an innovative and imaginative cook, dishing up cuisine such as game soup, sauce piquante, and rice *blancmange*. Not only did she sew clothes for the children, but she made for them fanciful dolls. She wove baskets, made quilts of brilliant colors and complex patterns, and created hand-tied lace curtains of unusual intricacy and gentility.

Being the acute observer she was, it is certain that the artistic atmosphere at Melrose—the constant swirl of writers and artists through the plantation halls and grounds, the roundtable discussions at mealtime, the tireless creative enthusiasm of Miss Cammie—had its impact on Hunter. By 1938, when François Mignon arrived at Melrose, she was primed for what would follow.

Mignon was the single most influential person in Hunter's artistic career. In the late 1930s, the native Frenchman had been engaged in foreign trade in New York City. During a particularly hot summer in the city, he and a boyhood friend decided to take a break and tour the Old South, renewing some old acquaintances along the way. Their Southern tour took them to Melrose Plantation, where they spent a weekend.

"It was a memorable weekend at Melrose," wrote Ora G. Williams in her introduction to Mignon's 1972 book, *Plantation Memo*. "But too many members of the family and guests from afar made it impossible for anyone to get very well acquainted. Returned to New York, Mignon found a letter awaiting him from Cammie Henry. It read: 'Dear François: So many people here the weekend you were. I got the impression you had too much sense to waste your life in the city. Come down and live in the country. Aunt Cammie.'"

A year later the war broke out in Europe and foreign trade came to a standstill. Mignon accepted the invitation and traveled to Melrose for an intended six-week visit.

Cammie Henry told Mignon that she desperately needed a curator for the plantation library, its collections, and her buildings and grounds. Lyle Saxon, who had served to some extent in that capacity for several years, had left Melrose to join the Federal Writer's Project. She needed a literary aid, a gifted writer such as he was, and a friend.

Mignon accepted her offer. He would remain at the plantation for thirty-two years, becoming "an elegant addition to this cultural household."

From his first encounter with Hunter, Mignon knew that she was something special. The day was a Saturday in early September, 1938. The occasion was a big birthday weekend for Saxon, who had made the trip up from Baton Rouge. Celebrants were crowded into every guest cabin on the grounds, and Clementine, having been one of Saxon's favorite servants while he was there, was pressed into service. Mignon recalled the occasion:

She was in service at the Big House for Miss Cammie, who had many guests that weekend. Mrs. Hunter was delegated to bring some afternoon coffee to Yucca House, for the gentlemen. The coffee was steaming hot and she put the coffee pot in the fireplace. And then she received instruction from Mr. Saxon that actually we didn't want any coffee, but we wanted some ice, and was there ice in the ice box? And there was, and she procured it for us. And then, as was his custom with the servants, Mr. Saxon suggested

Clementine Hunter and François Mignon arm in arm in front of the Yucca House, Melrose Plantation, 1978. Photo by B. A. Cohen.

that Mrs. Hunter might find some refreshments in the iron safe in his bedroom where he'd always kept his prized liquors. And Mrs. Hunter found that, and took the coffee pot and vanished. I never saw her again. . . . Until the next morning when she appeared to inquire if there wasn't something we all wanted, such as some of that coffee like we had yesterday . . . and there was a sly look in her eye when she mentioned "that coffee y'all had yesterday." . . . And I remember Mr. Saxon said, "What d'you mean, y'all? Didn't you get in on that party, too?" And she laughed and said, "Yas sir. But I had to take it home, 'cause Emanuel wouldn't like it if I had some and he didn't have none." So for that reason, and only that reason, she explained, she had taken some to Emanuel. Mr. Saxon liked to have Mrs. Hunter . . . because she understood him.

That first introduction in 1938 resulted in an intense communion of spirit between soon-to-be artist and mentor. And from that day until his death in 1980, Mignon would be an unwavering supporter of Hunter. Ora Williams' introduction to his chapters on Hunter in *Plantation Memo* suggests the extent of that support:

> Over the years, Francois promoted the artist's work by furnishing her materials—hundreds of boards and tubes of paint, by calling her paintings to the attention of critics and art dealers, by arranging for exhibitions of her work, by constantly writing about her in his columns, and by his never-flagging interest and encouragement. Her tremendous success as a primitive painter . . . can be in large part attributed to her long-time friend, François Mignon.

CHAPTER THREE

Beginning to Paint

HUNTER BEGAN PAINTING "about 1940," according to Mignon, although he once indicated that he thought she may have been "playing with paint" well before that time. Whether she had or not, the circumstances that drew her to her first canvas were very clear in Mignon's mind. He recorded the event in his writings:

> Well do I remember when Clementine Hunter, already many times a grandmother, first tried her hand at painting. Alberta Kinsey of New Orleans had been here painting magnolias, using the ante-bellum outside kitchen as her studio. Late one afternoon, following Miss Alberta's return to New Orleans, it fell to Clementine Hunter to tidy up the place. About 7 o'clock that evening, clutching a handful of discarded old tubes of paint, she tapped at my door, said that she could "mark" a picture on her own hook if she "sot her mind to it." Knowing her as I did, I figured she could do anything she "sot her mind to" and, with a view to aiding her in her enterprise, I cast about and came up with an old window shade, a few brushes and a dab of turpentine.
>
> At 5 o'clock the next morning, she tapped on my door again, explaining she had brought me her first picture. I took one look at it, nearly fell out at the sight of it and exclaimed: "Sister, you don't know it but this is just the first of a whole lot of pictures you are going to bring me in the years ahead."

From that moment she began to paint with zeal, her painting supplies coming from the riches of circumstance. She painted on anything she could find—cardboard boxes, the blank inside of soap cartons, brown paper bags, pieces of lumber, scraps of plywood, window shades—anything she or Mignon could lay their hands on. Her primary source of paint, early on, was still discarded tubes from visiting artists. Quickly, however, that source proved inadequate.

"She painted constantly," Mignon said. "Constantly. You couldn't stop her. It was terrible because at that time she didn't have any money." Mignon had little money himself, his role as plantation curator providing only staple support. But somehow he managed to come up with enough for an occasional mail-order purchase. "We got paints out of Sears and Roebuck" to keep her going, he said.

She painted most of her earliest pieces at night, often late at night. She had a full day's work at the Big House, and she was expected to take washing and ironing home to bring back the next day. At the same time she was taking care of Emanuel, whose health was rapidly deteriorating. It was not unusual for her painting to have to wait until midnight.

But no matter how tired she might have been, Hunter could not ignore this compulsion to paint. She would sit up all night, beside the dim glow of a coal oil lamp, "looking after Emanuel . . . and painting," recalled Mignon.

Another account, by longtime friends of the artist, demonstrates the depth of her quiet compulsion. Robert and Yvonne Ryan wrote:

> Clementine relates how, once, in the wee hours of the night as she was painting, her husband called from bed to say, "Woman, if you don't stop painting and get some sleep, you'll go crazy."
>
> "No," she replied. "If I don't get this painting out of my head I'll sure go crazy."

One of the clearest pictures of the Clementine Hunter of the early 1940s, when she was almost sixty years old, comes from James Pipes Register, a man who, along with Mignon, would help her make her first public bow. He wrote:

James Register, 1970. Photo from the Register Collection, Cammie G. Henry Research Center, Eugene P. Watson Library, Northwestern State University, Natchitoches, Louisiana.

At an early age Clementine became familiar with hard work. In her youth, and for many years afterwards, the workday was from sunrise to sunset and even later. Evidently the long hours of the workday instilled in Hunter little need for sleep or rest. "I don't like to sleep much," she explains. "I sleep a few hours, then lie there thinking about pictures, so I get up and start painting pictures."

If Mignon was the first source of spiritual support for Hunter the artist, James Register would become her first source of practical support. Register was an Oklahoma-based writer and occasional artist who traveled to Melrose in 1943 with an eye toward using the plantation's considerable library for research on a book about Louisiana. During his three-month stay he struck up a strong friendship with Mignon. Mignon in turn introduced him to Hunter and her works. He, like Mignon, was immediately taken by the woman, whom he would later call "Hunter the Visionary, Hunter the Artist and Hunter the Mysterious."

The two men spent hours cultivating her personal and artistic confidence, frequently walking the mile down to her cabin to spend a summer evening out on the gallery, just talking. Register was delighted by the riches of dialectic and colloquial offerings he found in the unaffected Hunter, and would often make notes of their conversations. His notes include these observations:

> Her fanciful expressions make up for her lack of education. She calls the highway "a navigating place." She speaks of her environment, "this is my native." When she rests, she says, "When I sits, I sits loose." Occasionally she has to use an eraser with her art work. She explains, "Sometimes the lines don't go right and I have to spoil them out." She refers to busy people, "They sure go 'round in a stir-up."

She returned his appreciation by addressing him in a personal but respectful way. She called him "Mr. Pipes."

Mignon wrote later that Register "has a finer perception of the artist's worth and has done more to inspire her than any other person." While that may not stand as entirely true throughout her career, there is little doubt that Register came along just at the right time.

There had never been more desperate times at the Hunter household. With Emanuel bedridden, Clementine was the sole provider. When Mignon had tried to rescue the family by getting them on the state "relief" rolls, he had been stalled by a bureaucratic point of order. And Hunter's artistic fever seemed to intensify correspondingly—the harder times got, the more she painted. Her demand for paints and supplies seemed ceaseless.

Register was by no means a wealthy man, but he was generous. After leaving Melrose and returning to his job at the University of Oklahoma, he set out to secure support for Hunter's art. He began sending her, through Mignon, small cash payments. He sent her boxes of paints, brushes, and art paper. And in less than a year he had secured for her a Julius Rosenwald Foundation Grant that would assist her "worthy artistic endeavor."

When Emanuel died in August of 1944, Register helped bear the funeral expenses.

Register continued to mail small cash payments and art supplies to Hunter after Emanuel's death. And in the meantime, he and Mignon began to collect her works and to cast about for opportunities to sell them—something the artist herself seemed reluctant to do, despite their encouragement.

She sold her earliest works, only when pressed, for twenty-five cents. "She was hesitant to tell me when she sold one," Mignon recalled. "She would say, 'Some people passed by and wanted my pictures. I had to sell them to them. They wouldn't go away unless I would.' She seemed to think she shouldn't sell them. She thought she was cheating people."

She preferred to give them away. She felt that once the picture was done, she was completely finished with it. So complete was her separation from the finished painting that she had no interest in negotiating a sale. Occasionally she would acknowledge that a picture "looked pretty good." Once in a while she gave one an "It'll do." Most often she would say nothing and just pass the painting off in the quickest, most convenient way.

Mignon and Register provided that convenience. Many of her earliest works fell to them, "in a casual Cane River sort of way," as Mignon referred to it. The Cane River way was simple and, to everybody's mind, equitable. Register sent Mignon money, art paper, and paints, which he delivered to Hunter; Mignon would pick up whatever pictures she had produced (often a dozen or more, indeed Mignon frequently expressed the worry that quantity would give way to quality); Mignon would package and mail some to Register in Oklahoma, and keep some for himself.

By early 1945, Register and Mignon had become more than just enthusiastic, earnest supporters. Suddenly they found themselves—perhaps by design, perhaps by accident—active collectors and agents of Clementine Hunter art. And whether Hunter saw it yet or not, they each had a vested interest. By the end of 1945, Register and Mignon would become full-fledged promoters of Hunter art.

Mignon, in his later writings, opined that Hunter's earliest works were her best. Register expressed the same opinion. Mignon also recalled her first paintings as simple, single-focus studies; prior to around 1944 she was "still dabbling with small items." He had said, too, that she produced a number of watercolors.

That she did work in watercolor at all, however, is suspect. It was her practice, in those early years, to stretch her painting supply as far as possible by thinning, often applying generous portions of turpentine. As a result, many of her early oils have the transparent quality associated with watercolors. Not to exclude the possibility, but if any watercolors do exist they are a rather well-guarded secret.

Mignon may also have been mistaken in his remembrance that the very first paintings were "small items." While it is difficult to date her earliest art—she neither dated nor signed her work in the early years—there is evidence that her first picture (or certainly among the very first) was a panoramic Cane River baptism, featuring more than a dozen figures, a river, a rectory, a church, and a graveyard. The painting, executed on a window shade, is a finely balanced, composed study of the human life cycle—particularly one very familiar to Hunter—and could hardly be considered simple.

It seems certain that the artist did not begin to sign her work until the late 1940s. Mignon gives conflicting accounts in his writings of when he instructed the illiterate artist on marking her initials on her work. One account would have her initialing paintings as early as 1941. Another suggests that she did not begin the practice until around 1955. Neither claim, however, holds up under close scrutiny, and it is likely that Mignon, drawing the accounts from distant memory, simply lost track of time.

The difficulty of precisely dating her first signed art is compounded by the appearance of a large number of paintings which are signed "Clemence" in Old English-style calligraphy, a calligraphy Hunter would have been totally incapable of even if she could have spelled her name. To be sure, the paintings are her work. They bear absolute resemblance to her unsigned

François Mignon and Clementine Hunter at Mignon's desk in Yucca House, Melrose Plantation (c. 1950). Photo from the Mignon Collection, Cammie G. Henry Research Center, Eugene P. Watson Library, Northwestern State University, Natchitoches, Louisiana.

works. And it is true that she insisted her name was originally Clemence and that she changed it after she moved to Melrose.

However, the most acceptable accounting for these paintings, and through it, a process for dating her first signed work, follows this line: Mignon and Register found the French "Clemence" more attractive from a "marketing" standpoint than Clementine, so the name was adopted for her signature. She being incapable of writing and Mignon's eyesight being poor, it fell to Register to affix the signature to the paintings—the unsigned ones she was sending him via Mignon in the years 1944–47. (The basis of this premise, and perhaps the best document of these early years in Hunter's painting career, is a series of letters from Mignon to Register written during 1944–45. The letters, which are essential to a full understanding of the relationship of the three, are included later in this book.)

What is certain is that a 1949 *New Orleans Item* review of her first public showing in Louisiana referred to the artist as Clementine, not Clemence. It is logical to assume (though not imperative) that her works were signed or initialed for the showing, and most likely that she would have been referred to by signature, or in the case of initials, by what they stood for. In any case, it appears that by 1949 the "Clemence" idea had been essentially abandoned. Paintings acquired directly from the artist in the very early 1950s bore the signature *CH*, a mark she would continue for nearly a decade.

CHAPTER FOUR

The Discovery
of an Artist

T HE APPEARANCE OF Hunter's paintings in the New Orleans Arts and Crafts Show of 1949 was the first to draw any critical attention. Not that she had gone without recognition until that time—certainly the 1945 Rosenwald Grant and small showings in Brownwood, Texas, and Waco, Texas, in the mid-1940s would attest to her growing reputation (and to the success of Register and Mignon in spreading her fame). But when *New Orleans Item* art critic Carter Stevens gave her work a three-paragraph review, he left little doubt that she had at last been discovered. He wrote:

> The most exciting discovery of the show, however, is Clementine Hunter, who lives up on Cane River. She is a primitive painter true and simple with a wonderful flare for colors and an intuitive grasp of composition.

Interestingly, the Stevens review was forwarded to Celeste Henry, the daughter-in-law of Cammie Henry, by Alberta Kinsey, the artist whose cast-off paints started Hunter's painting career. In a letter accompanying the review, Kinsey wrote:

> Dear Celeste, I am enclosing a clipping from the *New Orleans Item* with a review of the present show. Don't think he did justice to Clementine's pictures. They are the best here, especially the old church pictures. At least the artists say so.

When Stevens labeled Hunter a "primitive" painter, the die was cast. He had attached significance to her work, and he had begun to give it definition. For those who already enjoyed her art, it was confirmation. For skeptics, it was an invitation to look again. Slowly her paintings began to gain the attention of people outside her small circle of friends and patrons. However modestly, she was gathering steam.

Then, in the June 1953 issue of *Look* magazine, Charlotte Willard finished what Stevens had started. She gave full definition to the term "primitive painter," and in the process set Hunter down squarely amongst the most notable in the country. Referring to her works, and to those of several other artists, she wrote:

> The artists whose works appear on these pages are called "primitives." Unlike most painters who come to their art after many years of work, much gallery haunting and museum study, these natural painters rarely if ever sought art in museums or galleries. Self-taught, they came to painting late in life and they work as though nobody had ever before put color on canvas. The source of their art is not art but their own inner vision. . . . They all paint real things but they paint them from memory. The significant detail is magnified, the trivial, however big, is ignored. Their real people, their real flowers, their real landscapes have the reality of a dream, the emotional force and directness of a vivid personal adventure. The world on their canvases seems as wondrous and newly born as it does to the eyes of children, whose innocence these natural painters have by some happy miracle recaptured.

What followed the *Look* article was a burst of unprecedented recognition for a Southern black primitive artist. The recognition and the artistic accomplishment that accompanied it would run for several years. It would define a period in Hunter's creative life that must be considered some of her finest hours.

Almost simultaneously in mid-1955, two important galleries presented Hunter exhibitions. One, the Delgado Museum (now the New Orleans Museum of Art), offered its first one-man show by a black artist. The artist was Clementine Hunter. At the same time, Northwestern State College in Natchitoches held its first-

ever exhibit by its own native artist, Clementine Hunter. The latter exhibit was particularly significant because, while it was still ten years before the Civil Rights Act, the showing would enable the artist to see her work in a gallery for the first time.

She was not allowed to view her work with the white patrons, however, and without the help of a longtime friend may not have seen it at all. Ora Williams, who taught Greek literature at the college, recalled Hunter's first gallery viewing of her own work:

> I had to take her there on Sunday. The gallery was locked and nobody was there. I snuck her in through the back . . . she was so amazed. She didn't remember the paintings. She would throw her head back, laugh and say, "Where did you get that one . . . I don't remember that one." Gradually, it all came back to her.

While the two exhibitions set off a spate of local newspaper and television features of this "newly discovered" artist—and paved the way for many more such shows in the decades to come—Hunter was fast approaching one of the most important artistic undertakings of her life: the African House Murals.

The African House (c. 1800) is one of the most unique structures on the Melrose Plantation grounds. In its long history it served a variety of purposes. It is believed that it was originally a holding cell for recalcitrant slaves. Later it served as a provisions warehouse. At one time it was a nursery for baby chicks. Finally it had become a "glorified catch-all for plantation discards, including ante-bellum ploughshares, book cases, worn out furniture, saddles and saddlebags, and all the paraphernalia that generations of plantation life fall heir to," as Mignon described it.

Believed to be patterned after the African Congo huts in the ancestry of Marie Thérèse Coincoin, the two-story structure was built with brick baked on the plantation and thick hand-hewn cypress beams. Massive eaves extended ten feet beyond the exterior walls.

Mignon credits himself with the idea of the African House Murals and there is nothing to suggest otherwise. Doubtless, as curator of the plantation, he saw the melding of Hunter art with plantation history as a fitting tribute to each. It was in mid-1955, while attempting to "clear the African House of its accumulation of the ages," he said, that he came upon this idea: murals depicting all the color and pageantry of plantation life, filling the top floor of the plantation's most unique structure, painted by the plantation's own unique artist.

Hunter agreed to the project and within a week started work.

For the mural to encircle the room, it required nine large panels, each four by eight feet, and several small connecting panels. Each panel had to be painted separately, in studio space that Mignon had arranged there on the plantation grounds. The artist worked from a master sketch she had made which detailed how the sections must fall to make the whole, and what each should depict. The planning and painting took three months of full-time effort, according to Mignon's accounts. Plantation workers required another month to transfer, align, and permanently install the panels.

When viewed today, there is little doubt that the room, which has been described as "the most colorful room in the Old South," represents an artistic effort of large proportion. When one considers it the work of a sixty-eight-year-old woman, technically unskilled at painting, it stands even larger. But what is most impressive is the work itself: the unique, perceptive, gently humorous, virtually all-inclusive look at plantation life in Cane River Country, at the heart of which stood Melrose Plantation.

And while Mignon cannot be relied on entirely in his historical accounting—indeed he was a poet first and an historian later—his is the finest and most fitting description of the gallery he gave birth to. He described the murals in his newspaper writings:

> The first panel, centered on the north wall, is disc-shape in design. It is a pictorial map of the neighborhood stretching between Cane River and Red River, touched up by sketches of ante-bellum buildings. The map stresses the three main products of the plantation—cotton, pecans and churches, all three of which are produced in plenty.
>
> The second and third panels occupy the northwest corner and feature cotton culture. One of these panels is redolent of Spring, what with the field hands busy hoeing the tender new cotton while off to the left a wedding is in full swing.
>
> The companion panel depicts late summer or early autumn—the cotton being picked and weighed and over to the extreme right, a revival in progress, for the same heat that opens the cotton generates a quickening of interest in religion in Cane River Country. A swooning lady in this panel suggests that the religious fervor is reaching an impressive pitch.
>
> The fourth and fifth panels are situated in the southwest corner of the room. One represents a Cane River funeral as the procession moves from the church to the graveyard. Old Aunt Attie is riding on the hearse. She is about a hundred and loves funerals although she herself, consumed when fire destroyed her cabin a few years later, will never attend one of her own.
>
> The companion panel is striking enough. It started off as a baptisin' but ended up heading out for Heaven on a roller coaster when the artist lost her perspective. The whole composition is adrip with folklore and contains at least one feature that not even the artist realized she was

including. It came to my attention when a local citizen pointed to the lower right hand corner where an ancient car is parked by the margin of the river, from whence two ladies attending the festivities are proceeding on foot:

"Would them two ladies there be Jesus's sisters?" inquired the man viewing the picture for the first time. "I figure they all must be 'cause I notice they's a-walkin' on the water."

Panels six and seven grace the southeast corner. Here is as fine a mural of the primitive type as you are ever likely to encounter. It presents washday at the plantation and a clothesline on which plantation garments are flapping, including a pair of long red handlebars, a pair of yellow drawers with green lace and so on. For the most part, the gentlemen appearing in the composition are resting while all the ladies present are busily engaged in stirring the washpot, bending over the washtub and so forth. At the upper right, a self portrait of the artist, busy at her easel, rounds out the washday vignette.

The accompanying panel is primarily concerned with the pecan harvest, falling out of trees and all the rest. To the left, evening has descended upon the scene and, if you go far enough, you come to Heaven on earth on a plantation on Saturday night. It is the local honky-tonk where you will observe young gentlemen of color throwing dice, spilling a dab of wine, letting a little blood and generally disporting themselves while in the foreground an old sow with her little pigs moves ponderously in the direction of the river.

Panels eight and nine in the northeast corner round out the vibrantly colorful panorama of plantation life in Louisiana. In these two final panels, the artist incorporated three of the better known plantation buildings—Melrose, built in 1833, later the home of the late Mrs. Cammie G. Henry; Yucca, the original colonial residence, built in 1750; and the African House. Personalities associated with these buildings over the years also figure in these two final compositions, including Uncle Israel, the last surviving slave.

The story of the Cane River Country comes down to us and, in turn, is handed on to future generations in many different forms, not the least telling of which are the African House Murals.

On the completion of the murals, or soon after, Mignon and Hunter seized upon the artist's swelling popularity to explore another of her avenues of artistic expression: cooking. Melrose hospitality was by now legendary, and the food served its many distinguished guests was known as some of the best Louisiana had to offer. Hunter had won considerable fame during her years in the Melrose kitchen with her game soup, boiled bass, barbecued ham, sauce piquante, parsnip fritters, apple biscuits, brown bread, fig cakes, and puddings. If there ever was an opportunity to bring out a collection of her recipes, this was it.

While Hunter dictated her concoctions, Mignon typed them out. The result was a book called *Melrose Plantation Cookbook*, by Clementine Hunter and François Mignon. The success of the book added fuel to the Hunter phenomenon. And when one of the recipes was singled out by Alice B. Toklas for its originality, and accordingly registered with the French Academy in Paris, Hunter could call herself a blue ribbon artist in two fields.

By 1957, the now seventy-year-old artist had established herself as an important primitive/folk artist. Already she was being called the "Black Grandma Moses," or the "Grandmammy Moses," and the comparisons were beginning to hold up. Likewise Mignon had established himself as a fixture at Melrose Plantation. After Cammie Henry's death it had fallen to him to keep the red carpet out for artists, writers, and other important visitors. He had done a good job, and while the Henry family pursued its business interests, Mignon became the cultural voice of Melrose. Early in the year he found the perfect vehicle to perpetuate the tradition of Melrose and, in the process, the artistic career of Hunter.

On April 26, 1957, his first newspaper article, under his column head "Cane River Memo," appeared in the *Natchitoches Enterprise*. Not too long afterwards, other papers in the state began to feature his colorful accounts of plantation life at Melrose and of the notables who came to visit. He would write the column regularly for twenty-three years, until his death in 1980. Dozens of his articles were devoted entirely to Hunter.

Over the next few years, the artist continued to turn out often remarkable canvases. She had gathered a small but devoted local following, and she never wanted for art supplies. She had some years earlier begun drawing her "old age pension," and that, combined with the five to ten dollars she could demand for each new picture, kept her satisfied—and painting full-time.

She always insisted that she never worked to improve her style, though her works show a continuous evolution of artistic cunning and wit. She may have experimented with technique somewhat, but by the late 1950s, while still vivid and expressive with her brush, she was beginning to echo previously established patterns and themes. She was, in a sense, merely reproducing what she had already discovered.

There is no way of knowing, of course, where her work would have taken her had she continued along that path. But she did not, and there is every reason to believe that without the sudden infusion of new life that was to come she may not have extended her artistic reach much further.

Again it was Register who helped Hunter, this time making perhaps his most important contribution to her career. In 1962 he moved to Natchitoches permanently and rented a cabin on Cane River, just a few hundred yards from the artist's home. Register believed that Hunter was "almost a genius," based on his experiences with her in the late 1940s. And it was his expressed purpose, in 1962, to now "explore these talented and untapped treasures to see what limits" there were.

It was to be his grand experiment, and he described it in later writings:

A large bundle of old magazines was collected, the ads (all in diverse colors) were removed, but into an infinity of designs and patterns. Using heavy cardboards in sizes 16″×24″ through 22″×28″ the paper pieces were taped (with transparent tape) onto the board to form paper montages; flowers, people, animals, landscapes and the like.

These montages, along with painting-boards, were one at a time taken to Hunter along with large quantities of paints and brushes, bottles of turpentine and linseed oil.

The experiment was to determine to what extend the colored bits and pieces from the ads would jog her color sense and what translation she would give to these montages. The results were fabulous.

In two years time, she did in excess of a hundred large paintings. Many times she would use the montage to interpret it in her own way. Sometimes the montage would be so difficult, being only a series of color patterns, the outlines of the patterns would have to be traced on the board for her. But, even so, she did exquisite work on these considering there were scores of patterns and pieces on each board.

"They make my head sweat," she would say.

Probably, no professional artist could have done such magnificent work as she did. Eventually, the experiment having proved there was no limit to Hunter's prowess as an artist, the collection of over one hundred paintings were dispersed. Having paid Hunter for her work the paintings were broadcast to many outlets. Portions of the collection were given to Louisiana libraries, others were sold (and Hunter paid again if there were profits).

After this program was phased out, Clementine returned to satisfying the public demand for her primitives. The two-year montage period was an interesting one. It proved that Hunter's talents were like that of a fine musical composer that had to do ragtime for a living but could do epic compositions in which there are no limits!

Not only does Register's experiment account for the curious series of Hunter "abstracts" which appear seemingly out of nowhere, but it is the only incidence of a serious attempt to influence the artist's work. And while it may be arguable that Register's motives were something more than he admitted, it is undeniable that her subsequent works suddenly took on a renewed flash of spirit. Equally important is that, as Register dispersed these stunningly different Hunter works to collectors and patrons, it stirred a sharp new interest in her art.

The abstracts, too, help to date her works, establishing when she began making the backwards C in her signature. The abstracts all bear the backwards C, and knowing that these were executed in 1962–63 allows the assumption that she had already made the change by this time. Indeed, based on an examination of precisely dated acquisitions, it is almost certain that she began to sign her work ƆH, with the C separated from the H, in 1958.

Why she made this interesting little change is a mystery, and it has certainly been one of the mainstays of Hunter trivia. But the matter may not be as trivial as it seems. There are two prevailing explanations. The first is offered by Mignon, who cited the time she came to him and said:

> "Mr. François, do I have to make that C like that? 'Cause it look like to me if I take that C business and turned it around the other way, it'd be more friendly. . . . Look like if I got it this way [C], my back's up and I ain't friendly. But if I turned it around the other way it'd be friendly, and nicer."

The artist herself did not recall it that way. Contrary to Mignon's account, she maintained that she turned the C around as a practical matter. She had figured out that Cammie Henry and her daughter-in-law, Celeste Henry, also had the initials CH, and Hunter did not want there to be any question regarding who painted her pictures.

If Hunter's version is true—and it is difficult to argue with the source itself—it shows something of the artist that she did not often reveal: her fierce pride of authorship.

CHAPTER FIVE

The Later Years

F OR MUCH OF the century, culture rather than cotton had been king at Melrose Plantation. That era came to a close in 1970. Cammie Henry's son, J. H. Henry, Jr., had died the year before and it was decided by the heirs to put the magnificent plantation on the auction block. Everything would go: furnishings, buildings, grounds, and, of course, the people who had served it so well.

The plantation itself, including over twenty-five hundred acres, was purchased by Southdown Land Company. Its contents, including the numerous Hunter paintings that had dressed its various halls and buildings (except the African House Murals), were auctioned in a sale that would bring over fifty thousand dollars. Mignon, who had laid out its beautiful gardens, who had guided many visitors through the historic site, and who had so lovingly labored over Cammie Henry's scrapbooks of Louisiana history, was moved out of his thirty-two year residency at Yucca House. To his new residence in Natchitoches, which he named New Haven House, he took only his personal collection of Hunter paintings, his personal writings, and a few books.

However, the heritage of Melrose was not to be lost. Recognizing the history of the grand estate, Southdown the following year donated the eight buildings and the six acres of estate grounds on which they stood to the Association of Natchitoches Women for the Preservation of Historic Natchitoches. The African House Murals would remain in the public domain. In 1972, Melrose would go on the National Register of Historic Places, and in 1974, it would be declared a National Historic Landmark.

Hunter continued to live in her rented cabin just a short walk down the road from the Big House at Melrose.

The sale of the plantation, and the Hunter paintings it had held, served to stir again the public's interest in her art. Newspapers and magazines offered more features on the now almost ninety-year-old artist's landscapes of "the fast vanishing pageant that was plantation life in the South."

In 1971, Register authored and published a storybook illustrated by Hunter. The book, *The Joyous Coast*, immortalized Cane River with its "Qwan Qwan ducks"—Marie Thérèse's African name, Coincoin, was pronounced "qwan-qwan"—and paid tribute to the legend of Melrose. The book was an immediate success.

In 1974, Hunter's reputation had grown so—and with it, the price of her works—that the inevitable occurred: a forgery scare. Rumors that either a grandson or a nephew was grinding out Hunter copies and selling them began to fly. And in New Orleans, an artist was charged with copying her paintings and trying to sell them as Hunter originals.

Meanwhile, the demand for commissioned works continued to grow. More and more friends and patrons were calling on the artist for specific projects—something for a new kitchen in green and yellow, a Christmas card design, a decorative centerpiece for the waiting room at the office. The artist responded to as many requests as she could; the money was usually very good and the demands usually mild enough to allow her the creative latitude she needed. And while there were times when a buyer rejected a finished work—a color mismatch or a misunderstood subject—the artist never had difficulty selling the rejection to some hungry collector. She never kept any for herself.

During the 1970s, with Hunter originals numbering well into the thousands, large private and public collections began to spring up across the country. Her works were featured in major exhibitions from New York to California, at the rate of at least one and often several showings per year. In 1976, her work was included in the United Nations UNICEF calendar.

In 1979, Museum of American Folk Art director Robert Bishop said in his book, *Folk Painters of America*, "Clementine Hunter, of Melrose Plantation . . . is perhaps the most celebrated of all Southern contemporary painters."

By the late 1970s, Mignon's health had deteriorated and his eyesight was gone. Since his move into Natchitoches in 1970, some fifteen miles from Melrose, he had seen less and less of his friend, Hunter. And while he called her almost daily and continued to write about her in his newspaper columns, his assistance with painting supplies, with travel into town for commodities, with correspondence and even household chores, was no longer possible.

However, the cause to which he had given so much would not go neglected. In the early 1970s, a trio of Natchitoches residents began to do what Mignon no longer could. They were Thomas N. Whitehead, Dr. Mildred Hart Bailey, and Ann Williams Brittain.

Whitehead first met the artist in the late 1960s while still a student at Northwestern in Natchitoches. He bought first one painting, then another, and then another, until he found himself a Hunter collector, friend, and devotee. Soon after, as a public relations instructor at his alma mater, he began to help tend to her daily needs and to assume many of the public relations functions attached to her success. He became her media advisor, handled media appointments, and was even successful in coaxing the artist into granting interviews and attending at least a few of the growing number of functions being held in her honor.

Brittain had been a lifelong friend of the artist, tracing her relationship back through her mother's deep friendship with Hunter. (Her mother, Ora Williams, had been the one to sneak

Hunter into her first exhibit at Northwestern, in 1955. Too, she had provided Mignon with his New Haven House during the final ten years of his life.) Brittain became something of a social secretary for the artist, assisting Whitehead in arrangements for interviews and hosting social functions in her honor. She made weekly runs from the city down to Hunter's cabin, delivering supplies, groceries, and fan mail. And as an energetic traveler, she carried the Hunter flag into all parts of the country.

Bailey, who recalled seeing her first Hunter painting in a Natchitoches store in 1946, assumed the role of Hunter historian. With a representative Hunter collection well under way in 1970, she began the task of assembling the history of the artist and of maintaining a comprehensive bibliography. She wrote several nationally published articles on Hunter and in 1980 a monograph for a publication entitled *Four Women of Cane River*.

Bailey and Whitehead traveled extensively as lecturers on Hunter and her art. They served as guest curators for her shows across the country and contributed gallery notes for many of her major exhibitions.

The contributions of Whitehead, Bailey, and Brittain as benefactors, as ambassadors, as constant friends who were on call whenever they were needed were essential to the artist's success in the 1970s and 1980s. They, like Mignon, were among that small circle who saw Hunter's well-being as one of their noblest purposes. They remained at her service till her death.

In 1978, Hunter left her cabin near Melrose. The familiar sign which had hung on her porch so many years—"Clementine Hunter, Artist, 50¢ to look"—came down for good. The historical association which was to preserve Melrose had made arrangements to move her cabin onto the grounds behind the Big House, and to make it a permanent part of the historic landmark.

The ninety-one-year-old artist was moved upriver to a quiet plot of land away from the rush of tourists and well-intentioned visitors. She moved into a trailer home which she bought with earnings from her paintings.

In 1980, at the age of eighty-one, Mignon died following a stroke. He was buried in mausoleum space he had purchased at St. Augustine Church, just down the road from Melrose. His last will had been very specific. He was to be buried next to the space which had already been purchased by a friend of his, Clementine Hunter.

In 1983, at the age of seventy-one, Register died. He was buried in Natchitoches. He had had to sell his entire collection of Hunter paintings to make ends meet during his last years.

Register, like Mignon, left no heirs. Each had spent his final years in modest surroundings and amongst only a very small circle of friends. Oddly, the two were not close friends at the last. Their importance to Hunter's artistic career, however, cannot be overlooked. And it is perhaps fate's unkindness that they did not live to see the extent to which she would be honored in the 1980s.

In 1980, Radcliffe College concluded and published a five-year Black Women Oral History Project which featured Hunter. Radcliffe's accompanying photographic exhibition, *Women In Courage*, also included her. In 1981, Illinois State University sponsored a six-state traveling exhibition featuring Hunter art. In 1982, a two-year effort to restore and preserve the African House Murals began, funded by Dr. Hugh Schoephoerster, an avid collector. In 1984, while financial articles were advising that Hunter paintings were "appreciating investments," the artist's works were being seen in exhibitions in New York City, Washington, D.C., and other major cities.

In 1986, Hunter received what was perhaps her most distinctive honor. Thirty-one years after she had seen her paintings in a gallery for the first time, the university which had offered that exhibit bestowed upon her the degree of Honorary Doctor of Fine Arts. It was only the fourth honorary doctorate issued by the hundred-year-old institution, Northwestern State University.

Hunter attended her doctoral ceremonies in a black cap and gown. A gold tassel hung among the black ringlets of her hair, specially done for the occasion. Her rhinestone earrings sparkled. Upon receipt of the degree she looked out into the audience of more than a thousand friends and admirers, into the glare of photographers' lights, and said simply, "Thank you."

In 1987, Hunter was one hundred years old. She continued to make efforts to paint throughout most of the year, though it was often physically difficult and only for painfully brief moments.

In early December, as a particularly harsh winter began to set in, her fragile health worsened. She was confined to her bed. She could no longer paint at all.

On January 1, 1988, the years took her away; she died of what her doctors called, in simple terms, old age. Beside her bed were family and friends.

On January 6, 1988, she was laid to rest near Melrose, in mausoleum space beside her dear old friend, François Mignon.

Clementine Hunter at ceremonies awarding her the Honorary Doctor of Fine Arts, at Northwestern State University, Natchitoches, Louisiana, 1986.

Works by Category

CLEMENTINE HUNTER CREATED several thousand paintings in her career. She left her mark on a variety of surfaces. In addition to canvas, board, and paper, she created images on everything from snuff bottles, to wine jugs, to gourds, to black iron skillets. Virtually anything that would hold paint could hold a Hunter painting. Additionally, she made a number of outstanding quilts which carry the familiar Hunter scenes.

The artist saw the cost of a finished work go from as little as twenty-five and fifty cents in the early 1940s, to one dollar in the late 1940s and 1950s, to three dollars in the early 1960s, to hundreds of dollars in the 1970s and thousands of dollars in the 1980s. She sold every piece she ever produced, with the exception of a very few works that were given to family and close friends.

While her subjects are repeated again and again, no two are exactly alike. The composition and the colors may be very similar, particularly in later works, but virtually every painting still carries its own distinctive marking.

Hunter rarely titled her work, though when pressed by a purchaser she may have described what the painting was about. "That's pickin' cotton," she might say of a picture of six black women in a cotton field. Largely, titles that have been assigned to Hunter paintings have been done so, as a practical matter, by their owners.

While by no means a full accounting, the majority of her works may be divided into four broad categories: Work, Play, Religion, and Other. Within those categories there are main themes and variations on them. Below are her most popular and prevalent themes listed by category.

WORK

Picking Cotton, Hoeing Cotton, Hauling Cotton,
    Ginning Cotton
Gathering Gourds
Gathering Pecans
Harvesting Sugarcane
Slaughtering Hogs
Raising Children, Babies
Washday
Work Collages (panoramas of plantation work)

PLAY

Saturday Night at the Honky Tonk
Going Fishing, Fishing, Fish Fry
Playing Cards
Eating Watermelon
Cooking in the Yard
Dancing

RELIGION

The Nativity, Mary and Baby Jesus on the Donkey
Weddings
Baptizings
Funerals and Wakes
Going to Church
The Crucifixion
Angels Flying
The Flight into Egypt

OTHER

Zinnias
Pinwheel Spider Lilies
Butterfly Lilies
Birds
Uncle Tom in the Garden
Cane River Ducks
Cats Sitting in the Grass
Chickens
Melrose Auction, The Big House, African House, Yucca House
Ladies in Calico
The Masks (a series)
Abstracts (the James Register series)
Going to School, The Schoolhouse
The Hospital, The Doctor
The Courtroom

Dating Hunter Paintings by Signature

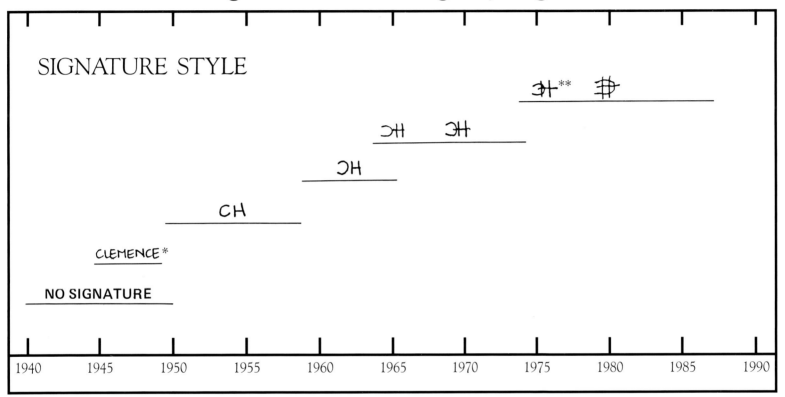

The above chart provides a way to date Clementine Hunter paintings by signature. Some signature periods overlap slightly because exact dating of her changes in style has proven nearly impossible. However, based on a study of a large number of precisely dated acquisitions, these periods can be considered essentially reliable.

* Some Hunter paintings were signed "Clemence" by James Register during the period 1944–47.

** In the mid-1970s the artist began moving her "Ɔ" into her "H" until it was superimposed completely, "⩐".

Clementine Hunter. From the Mildred Bailey Collection, Natchitoches, Louisiana.

COLOR PLATES
AND ARTIST'S COMMENTARY

Clementine Hunter, 1974. Photo by John C. Guillet.

Pencil sketch, dated 1939 but probably actually executed about 1949, canvas. (Courtesy Jack and Ann Brittain and children)

Quilt, sewn in 1938, size 4½ feet by 6 feet. (Mildred Hart Bailey Collection)

AT RIGHT:
Calinda Corvier Was Over One Hundred Years Old, painted about 1940, oil on windowshade. (Courtesy Dr. and Mrs. Robert Ryan)

Madam Carencrow Sitting Upon Her Nest, painted about 1944, oil on paper. (Courtesy Dr. and Mrs. Robert Ryan)

Green Lilies, painted about 1944, oil on black paper. (Courtesy Dr. and Mrs. Robert Ryan)

PM Gave Me This Orange Pitcher, painted about 1944, oil on black paper. (Courtesy Dr. and Mrs. Robert Ryan)

AT LEFT:
Trying to Keep the Baby Happy, painted about 1944, oil on paper. (Courtesy Dr. and Mrs. Robert Ryan)

One of the Rogers Boys on a Horse, painted about 1944, oil on paper. (Courtesy Dr. and Mrs. Robert Ryan)

Ducks, painted about 1945, oil on paper. (Courtesy Dr. and Mrs. Robert Ryan)

AT RIGHT:
Feeding the Chickens, painted 1948, oil on paper. (Courtesy Jack and Ann Brittain and children)

She's Not Pretty but She's Strong, painted 1948, oil on paper. (Courtesy Jack and Ann Brittain and children)

Cane River Washday, painted 1949, oil on paperboard. (Courtesy Jack and Ann Brittain and children)

AT LEFT:
Going to the Cotton Gin, painted about 1950, oil on paperboard.
(Courtesy Jack and Ann Brittain and children)

Statue of Black Man, called *The Good Darkie Statue* when this was
painted about 1950, oil on cardboard. (Courtesy Jack and Ann
Brittain and children)

AT LEFT:
Gathering the Figs, painted about 1950, oil on paperboard. (Courtesy Jack and Ann Brittain and children)

Gourds, painted about 1950, oil on paperboard. (Courtesy Jack and Ann Brittain and children)

BAPTIZING

That's the baptizing. They is going to church. That's the way they used to do, long time ago. Baptize down there in the lake. Not in front of the church—further from the church, other side of the bridge. That's the little children they gonna baptize.

Baptizing, painted about 1950, oil on paperboard. (John C. Guillet Collection)

Cutting Board (Thomas N. Whitehead Collection)

Hog Killing, painted about 1950, oil on paperboard. (Courtesy Jack and Ann Brittain and children)

AT RIGHT:
Mary, Baby Jesus, and the Three Wise Men, painted about 1950, oil on paperboard. (Courtesy Jack and Ann Brittain and children)

AT LEFT:
Funeral, painted about 1950, oil on paperboard. (Courtesy Jack and Ann Brittain and children)

Wake, painted about 1950, oil on paperboard. (Courtesy Jack and Ann Brittain and children)

SCHOOL

I quit school when them people just fight all the time and choked them school children. You see, the white children and the colored children was joining together, they had a fence between us, you know, our school on this side, the white school on that side. And they just choke them children and fight them children and I'd run off and I tell it to Sister Benedict.

Sister Benedict that was my teacher and she was mean and I tell her, I say, "Sister, can I go and get some water?" and she say, "Yeah, go ahead and hurry back and get to your lesson." And that put her all right, and I hurry back. And before she know one thing, I had done gone to the cistern to get water and done jumped the fence and gone home. Mama would whip me and make me come back with her, go back again and run off again, never did learn nothing. I told Mama I'd rather go back in the field. You know I was crazy, 'cause I'd rather go in the field and work, I'd rather go pick cotton. And I didn't learn nothing. I went and pick cotton.

Later I went to night school, that when Papa and them first moved to Melrose. That's when them old people, they all dead, what used to teach school, at night . . . that was some of my husband people. I didn't learn nothing there. I went to school every night, just running in the moonlight, I didn't learn nothing. I didn't want to learn nothing.

Graduation, painted about 1950, oil on paperboard. (Courtesy Jack and Ann Brittain and children)

Wood Watermelon Slice (Thomas N. Whitehead Collection)

Funeral, painted about 1955, oil on paperboard. (Courtesy Jack and Ann Brittain and children)

AT RIGHT:
Wedding, painted about 1955, oil on cardboard. (Courtesy Jack and Ann Brittain and children)

PAINTING

I paint just everytime I wasn't doing nothing. I'd pick up something, sometime I was going down the road and see a board what I could paint on, I'd pick it up and paint on that, I didn't know. And then when I'd paint, I'd give it away. I didn't think, you know, it was worth nothing to keep and I'd just give them away. I just like to paint, they be just give me the paint and I just like to paint . . . I paint at night. I mark my pictures at night. Get a pencil and mark them by the lamplight. Things would come to my mind, well, I'd mark them. . . . It just get in my mind and I just go ahead and paint but I can't look at nothing and paint. No trees, no nothing. I just make my own tree in my own mind, that's the way I paint. . . . When I'm painting it just gets in my mind what I ought to paint, look like it say, "You ought to paint this." Well, I just go ahead and paint that, that's all. But I can't go ahead, somebody go tell me what to paint, and show me how to do it, I can't do that.

I don't enjoy nothing much, but painting. Don't go nowhere. Anytime I start, I just go ahead and finish. I don't go to dances, don't go to ball games, or nothing, just stay home.

Melrose Complex, painted about 1955, oil on paperboard. (Mildred Hart Bailey Collection)

Recipe Box (Thomas N. Whitehead Collection)

DEATH OF FRIENDS, LOVED ONES

All the good people gone. Sometime you can lay down in the bed at night and think about all that. The Lord got them so they don't think about it, but just now and then it run across the people mind. The good Lord died for us, we got to die for Him. He sure died for us.

Funeral, painted about 1955, oil on paperboard. (Mildred Hart Bailey Collection)

Key Chain (Thomas N. Whitehead Collection)

80   CLEMENTINE HUNTER

AT LEFT:
Clouds, painted 1956, oil on paperboard. (Mildred Hart Bailey Collection)

One Panel of the African House Murals at Melrose Plantation, painted 1956, oil on plywood. (Courtesy Association for the Preservation of Historic Natchitoches)

AT LEFT:
Flowers, painted 1962, oil on canvas board. (Courtesy Dr. and Mrs. Robert Ryan)

Alice in Wonderland, painted 1962, oil on canvas board. (Courtesy Dr. and Mrs. Robert Ryan)

Zinnias in the Black Planter, painted 1962, oil on paperboard. (Courtesy Dr. and Mrs. Robert Ryan)

Yellow Bowl of Flowers, painted 1962, oil on canvas board. (Courtesy Dr. and Mrs. Robert Ryan)

Abstract, painted 1963, oil on canvas board. (Mildred Hart Bailey Collection)

Abstract, painted about 1963, oil on paperboard. (Mildred Hart Bailey Collection)

SATURDAY NIGHT AT THE HONKY TONK

It's the Saturday night. That the Melrose place, down there, I call it Metoyer place.

That's a fan in the window. That man down there drunk. And they [two ladies] fighting there. They fighting over that man, I reckon.

This one shot this one, and he stabbed this one in the back, see there . . . and this one out here drinking and he, instead of him pulling the bottle out her [the lady in red dress] mouth, he hit it with his fist and broke it, you see that. I know it hurt her. . . . And he pouring her a drink . . . she fell out yonder drunk, she fell out drunk. And look the bottle on the side. And they shooting at that man yonder. And look behind the tree, now he falling out. The lady in blue is wiping her mouth, trying to get her through—she drunk. Under the tree, that's what you call a drunkard there. She got a fifth sitting on her lap, and she have her glass with her and that man standing behind her, he drinking.

They don't hardly drink [today] like they used to drink. They don't fight like they used to, fighting and shooting. They don't do that much no more, but they does it, but not often.

That was a big fight, everybody they had fun, when they wasn't running . . . from the bullet . . . people be shooting all around that place, but I tried to get out the way.

I went there one night, one Saturday night, and they was shooting so much all over the place, when I did got out of that place, I fell down, and when I fell, I got up, you talk about running . . . I never did went back no more, never get a chance to kill me in that place.

I used to like to hear them play the music and I used to go there and drink my head off, I used to drink it, too, but I never make no racket or nothing when I drink. After that I betcha I got my drinking and stay to my house, no went back there no more.

Saturday Night at the Honky Tonk, painted 1963, oil on canvas board. (Mildred Hart Bailey Collection)

Black Iron Pot (Thomas N. Whitehead Collection)

Uncle Tom, painted 1963, oil on canvas board. (Courtesy Dr. and Mrs. Robert Ryan)

Zinnias, painted about 1965, oil on masonite. (Courtesy Jack and Ann Brittain and children)

Washday, painted about 1965, oil on paperboard. (Courtesy Jack and Ann Brittain and children)

Trixie's Zinnias, painted about 1965, oil on canvas board. (Mildred Hart Bailey Collection)

Fishing on Cane River, painted 1965, oil on canvas board. (Mildred Hart
Bailey Collection)

94   CLEMENTINE HUNTER

BLACK JESUS

That's Black Jesus, and the angel[s] . . . I don't know if [they] black or white. 'Cause nearly everybody says "Black Jesus," so I thought I'd make him black like.

Black Jesus, painted 1965, oil on canvas board. (Courtesy Dr. and Mrs. Robert Ryan)

High Mass, painted 1969, oil on canvas. (Courtesy Dr. and Mrs. Robert Ryan)

AT RIGHT:
Two Sisters, painted 1969, oil on paperboard. (Courtesy Dr. and Mrs. Robert Ryan)

NATIVITY SCENE

That's Mary and the Baby Jesus, and the . . . angels, and the three wise men taking her a present. One of them got a cake, and one got a gourd, and one got a present in the box—it be candy or cake. I just call that just the little red house. That's their house, . . . that's the baby's house.

They're not a special tree . . . I just make them trees. See the angels flying up in the air. That their hair flying up like that.

Nativity Scene, painted about 1970, oil on paperboard. (Thomas N. Whitehead Collection)

Snuff Bottles (Thomas N. Whitehead Collection)

100   CLEMENTINE HUNTER

PICKIN' COTTON

I was about fifteen or sixteen when I pick cotton. I would pick now, if I could. It was easy to pick. You pull the sack, you know, until it get heavy. When it get heavy, you empty it, pick some more, empty that.

I couldn't pick no dew cotton. You know in the morning, early, that cotton full of dew and I couldn't pick that. I had to wait. It wasn't too heavy, it just stick on my hands, I wait until the dew dried, then I pick cotton. I was done about five o'clock, I reckon. The sun was way up yonder then.

Put my children under the tree in the field. Pick cotton, 150 pounds, sometimes 200, I pick. All that was fifty cents a hundred, that's all they was getting. Fifty cents a hundred and I done dragged my children all in the field. I didn't have no baby-sitters like they do now. All of them got to have baby-sitters. Mine sat in the field, at the end of the row. Sometime I'd find some of them fast asleep in the weeds. They never die, I raise them all, too . . . had a time. I no paint that.

I work hard in my days. That's how come I got to keep a working. 'Cause I don't feel like I could, I don't think I could just quit it all, not just sit down, I can't, I got to do a little something, have to do a little something.

Pickin' Cotton, painted 1973, oil on wood. (Geoffrey J. Wilson Collection)

Brittain Family Portrait (from photo), painted 1975, oil on canvas board. (Courtesy Jack and Ann Brittain and children)

AT RIGHT:
Pecan Threshing, painted about 1975, oil on canvas board. (Thomas N. Whitehead Collection)

UNCLE TOM IN THE GARDEN

That's Uncle Tom in the garden and his little house. That's a shovel, he's digging on it and that's the little girl that be with him and her pet goose. That's that little girl's pet goose; see that goose got her dress tail, he pulling on her dress tail, and that them birds, the birds flying over the flower garden.

That's a little garden.

That's a bird house. . . .

She just name anything; I name her Mary. Mary and the goose.

Uncle Tom in the Garden, painted about 1975, oil on canvas board. (Mildred Hart Bailey Collection)

Plastic Milk Jug (Thomas N. Whitehead Collection)

Christmas Tree, painted about 1975, oil on paperboard. (Thomas N. Whitehead Collection)

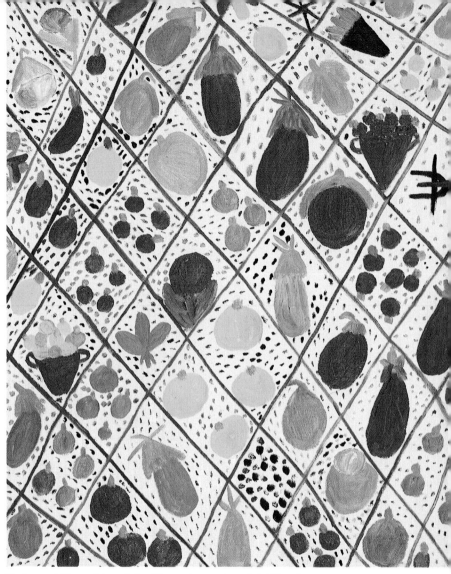

Fruits and Vegetables of the Plantation, painted 1975, oil on canvas board. (Thomas N. Whitehead Collection)

AT RIGHT:
It's Tour Time, painted about 1975, oil on paperboard. (Thomas N. Whitehead Collection)

106   CLEMENTINE HUNTER

MONEY/DEBT

I don't like to borrow, and if I borrow I know I got to pay and it just worry me, you know. I been like that. I got behind on my car one time and I swear to God I like to took a fit. My children say, "Oh, Mama, you don't got to worry," but shoot, I worry, I'm not like them.

Never did like to go nowhere and ask nobody for nothing. I hate it, and if I borrow something from somebody, I just, look like I just hate it if I can't pay them right away. That's how come I don't like to borrow. 'Cause look like that just stay on my mind, stay on my mind. I got to pay them. But some people can owe you and don't never pay, pass by you and scared to look 'cause they owe you. I don't do that. I can't. I can't. Sometime I don't have a nickel. Sometime I don't have a nickel to get my gas, got to wait, you know, until I make it, and then pay them. I just stayed there without it, I didn't ask nobody. Sometimes you borrow something and you think you can pay it and you can't. Maybe someday I go borrow something and that the very time I can't paint nothing, then what am I going to sell? Can't sell one unless I paint, and that's what I worry about.

The Buildings at Melrose, painted about 1975, oil on paperboard. (Thomas N. Whitehead Collection)

Glass Bottle with Brushes (Thomas N. Whitehead Collection)

MARRIAGE

I was scared when I got married. . . .

I didn't see marrying nobody what gonna keep me out of the field. I marry somebody what going to put me right straight on in the field. But I had a good husband, though. I had a good husband and a good Christian husband and he loved to work and he loved to have something. He always wanted to have something. Didn't want to never be without nothing. And just like that I'm is right now.

Wedding, painted 1976, oil on canvas board. (Thomas N. Whitehead Collection)

Wood Purse (Thomas N. Whitehead Collection)

Courtroom, painted 1976, oil on canvas board. (Mildred Hart Bailey
Collection)

Card Playing, painted about 1978, oil on canvas board. (Thomas N. Whitehead Collection)

Moving Day, painted 1978, oil on canvas board. Private collection.

AT RIGHT:
Arc En Ciel, painted 1979, oil on canvas board. (Mildred Hart Bailey Collection)

WORK

I used to farm, hoe cotton, hoe corn, grow sugarcane, pick cotton, done all that. Some people say work will kill you. Work don't kill nobody, but you ain't got to work till you kill yourself. But work ain't gonna kill no one. Work, I tell you what work will do. Work will keep you from begging, get you something to eat, and some clothes. But if you sit down and don't work, don't do nothing, everything you want, ask somebody else for it—uh uh. I'm sure glad I wasn't raised like that. No, my mama and daddy raised us to work, and my daddy used to work until it look like he generally had no sense. And my husband too, what die, he work.

I don't see how some people can sit down and rather steal than to work. No, I ain't gonna steal nothing from nobody what got. If I want something that somebody got, they ain't got but two words to say. I ask them for it; they can either say yes or no, and I be through with that. Uh huh. But some people rather go take something, knowing after them, that's what they're doing all over the world right now. But since I don't do it, that's all right. Yeah, what somebody else do, let them go ahead.

Plantation Harvest, painted 1979, oil on canvas board. (Mildred Hart Bailey Collection)

Snuff Bottle (Thomas N. Whitehead Collection)

Mary Pregnant (first in a series of two), painted 1980, oil on canvas board. (Mildred Hart Bailey Collection)

Mary with Child (second in the series), painted 1980, oil on canvas board. (Mildred Hart Bailey Collection)

The Moon and Stars, painted about 1980, oil on canvas board.
(Thomas N. Whitehead Collection)

AT RIGHT:
Christmas Wreath, painted 1980, oil on canvas sheet. (Thomas N.
Whitehead Collection)

AT LEFT:
Couple Dancing, painted about 1980, oil on paperboard. (Courtesy Jack and Ann Brittain and children)

Chicken Hauling Flowers, painted about 1980, oil on canvas board. (Courtesy Jack and Ann Brittain and children)

ANGELS

That's the angels. I call them [in red] the devil. That's what I say it is. They fly around to try to gain their soul. They got lot of them die young, a lot of children, die young.

Their robes, it's flying you know. When they flying in the air, their hair got to go.

I hope I will be an angel, I'm gonna try hard to be one, try hard. Look like everybody ought to try to be an angel, but everybody happy now. They're going somewhere else, they got to go somewhere. Some of them die drunk and some of them just die all at once.

Angels, painted about 1980, oil on paperboard. (Thomas N. Whitehead Collection)

Snuff Bottle (Thomas N. Whitehead Collection)

Hospital, painted 1983, oil on canvas board. (Mildred Hart Bailey
Collection)

Cat in the Grass, painted 1985, oil on canvas board. Private collection.

AT LEFT:
Sick Old Man in the Half Tester Bed, painted 1987, oil on canvas board.
(Thomas N. Whitehead Collection)

Zinnias, painted 1987, oil on canvas board. (Thomas N. Whitehead Collection)

Washday, painted 1987, oil on canvas board. (John C. Guillet
Collection)

The Letters
of François Mignon

THE FOLLOWING ARE excerpts from letters written by François Mignon to James Register during 1944 and 1945. At the time, Register was living in Norman, Oklahoma, where he worked at the University of Oklahoma, and Mignon was living on Melrose Plantation, where he was curator. Less than a year before these letters begin, Register had visited Melrose and Mignon had introduced him to Clementine Hunter.

Many years after the letters were written, and after Hunter had been established as an important folk artist, Register excerpted from the original letters only those portions pertaining to Hunter. Perhaps he intended to publish them as a collection. Or possibly he intended them for inclusion in a book he would write on her. In any case, they are published here for the first time.

In 1970, Register allowed Mildred Hart Bailey to copy his excerpts for her growing reference library on the artist. Those included here are from that library and are essentially intact, although some editing has been done in the interest of space and clarity. Several long excerpts which seemed repetitious have been omitted altogether. A few people referred to in the letters have never had their relationship to Hunter clearly identified.

The letters offer a pleasant inside look at the relationship of Hunter to Mignon and Register. Too, they provide a genuine feeling for the culture in which she lived and worked, thanks to Mignon's wonderful epistolary prose. And finally they show how the two men came to Hunter's assistance in the early years of her career, to encourage, to cultivate, and to promote her art.

August 8, 1944

Saw Miss Hunter last night after dark. Couldn't distinguish very clearly, but viewed many examples of her handiwork. Miss H. says she has need of white paint and of orange. She and her husband had many a nice word concerning you and she is looking forward to surprising you with many a fine piece when they have dried and we can get them done up for you.

August 22, 1944

I called on Clemance. Before she would talk, she ransacked the house for the pictures. There must be some forty odd—and I will send them along as soon as things are a little more in order. Aside from the big house, my time is being devoted to the Relief Office, where I hope to get things fixed up for Clemance. It will require a trip up there, I believe. Clemance says she is going to move from her present house to the last house on Shoo-shoo Lane, two houses below the inception of the road where Sam Browne lives. Her son, King, lives on that Lane, too. Clemance's husband died early Sunday morning. He will be buried tomorrow [Wednesday].

August 23, 1944

I passed by Clemance's house where the wake was in full flower. Her face betrayed nothing of her feelings when others sobbed a little. Her husband was laid out in the front room. The casket was placed across the north-east corner of the room, just under her bulletin board. There were no recent sketches decorating the walls, for they had gone forward to you. A candelabra with eight candles flamed in the slight breeze at the foot of the casket. A white netting over the body was raised so that I might observe. Perhaps twenty women sat in chairs in a circle about the room. The men sauntered in the dark outside. Often this one or that one would inquire after you, expressing the wish that you might have been present. There was some frolicking by the fourteen and fifteen year olds—especially the girls, but for the most part things were subdued. People spoke in hushed tones. The atmosphere rocked with something or other that was probably the mere concentration of so many personalities of distinction in one place. Having administered Extreme Unction, the Catholics thought they had the situation well in hand, but when Clemance learned that they wouldn't say anything in the Church, but merely bury Emanuel in the graveyard, she put her foot down. Accordingly at ten this morning, the Baptists at St. Matthews will take over. So runs Cane River current.

August 30, 1944

I delivered Clemance's paints. She is still attacking her picture business madly,—although it was too dark for me to examine. I suggested she do a painting of the wake for you. She licked her chops at that idea. I reckon there will be further items to forward to you shortly. I am having a little difficulty regarding the Relief Business. The office insists,—and I guess they are right,—on her having her birth certificate. She has in the offing, at least, a baptismal certificate, which will do as well. It is in the Catholic records in Cloutierville. She is going down there to get it this week. If I can, I should like to effect this immediately, since Clemance's daughters are screaming at her to come to Texas. I have given her some money to help hold her here while the Relief thing is stewing, but I didn't have as much as I would have had could it have been possible. But I think it will help keep her provisioned here for a while,—and in the meantime I am hoping so.

September 1, 1944

After too many days of rain, I got down to Miss Hunter's house last night about first dark. I took the snap-shots along. There was a light in the house and I found Miss H. painting madly. "That's pure me!" exclaimed Miss H., as she took one look at the first photograph. If I had only had your note book and pencil with me, I could have taken down a flock of good lines. As I left, Miss H. said be sure to tell him, "We love the pictures." It was the first time I had ever heard Miss H. using that phrase. She has done a flock of pictures which I tried to make out as best I could by lamp light. She wants me to send them to you this coming week. One of a man sitting under a tree in complete relaxation and shooting at birds in an adjoining tree, bearing flowers bigger than the birds, is quite striking. Another of a man with a stick about a foot long, about to strike at two huge gorillas in the bushes, is equally arresting. Miss H. explained that "That man, I say, jus' run up on them two varmints when he was out walking." I reckon gorilla is a word she hasn't heard,—and perhaps has never seen one of those animals. She said that "them varmints" just streaked across her mind.

September 12, 1944

I think it would help Miss H. out a great deal if you could arrange to send her a little money from time to time, and to it I shall add what I can. As Jackie reads, you might send the money directly to Miss H., and her daughter can explain the meaning of the contents. If this were sent in check form,—say a couple of dollars at a time, she could have the check cashed up at Ashely's store. If, on the other hand, you would rather send the money through me, you might just register the envelope, and Bill would hand it to me directly, and I could pass it along. I know she is quite short of money at the moment, for the last relief check, which we got cashed, was all eaten up to the last cent by indebtedness consequent to Emanuel's last days of illness and his burial. She has been held up about getting her baptismal certificate because of the cost of transportation to Cloutierville plus the cost the Reverend Father down there charges for the service. I have helped her when I could, but what with other demands, the Cloutierville trip hasn't seemed possible to her as yet. I think with what can be gathered together this week end, she may make the trip early in the week. Once the date of her baptism is established, we shall see exactly what progress can be made toward establishing the relief business.

September 14, 1944

The new supply of paper arrived in yesterday's mail and without delay I took it down the road. The lady of the brush was enchanted. She told me of three white ladies who had called from one of the camps owned by an Alexandria family. It seems one of the ladies was an artist, or at least was studying art. She asked our girl friend to come to Alexandria to study with her. Our girl friend declared she didn't have to go to learn something from anybody because God was putting in her mind how to do things. She also told the lady that she didn't want to paint flowers that she looked at because God made the flowers grow in her own mind and that she wanted to paint them and not the ones that merely grow in the ground. The lady told her she would send her some paint if she would give her a picture, but Miss H. declared she had no need of paint, as she always had everything she wanted. Mary Frances' papa and the latter's sister write from California about prosperity out there, where Mary Frances' aunt is currently receiving $13.50 a day as a lady riveter,—but Miss H. says "I know here and I don't know yonder," so it appears she will stick to her wash tubs and her paint brush and let him who will rivet, rivet. I brought back with me a number of examples of the lady's handiwork. Some interested me,—some did not. These will go forward to you today. I looked at them in the dark the other evening, and shall not unwrap them probably before taking them over to the office. It seemed to me the cotton pickers on black paper was one of the more interesting, and the vase of flowers on the little tabouret was equally so. I am so fascinated by the very distinctive shape of Miss H.'s umbrellas that I feel we ought to do some sort of a thing in which it would be appropriate for an umbrella to appear in every illustration.

October 6, 1944

I have been down to see Miss H.,—taking with me the package of colored paper that came through nicely. I found the lady, although after bed time, working away madly on picture after picture . . . the sheets of tossed off compositions lay about on the floor like autumn leaves in a winter's wind. I glanced at some of them, but am scarcely prepared to say if I had anything save a blurred impression. I am afraid I must put on the brakes more heavily, since quantity is still running ahead of quality as a prime consideration.

October 9, 1944

The check has gone to Clemance. I have a batch of pictures, and these will go forward either today or tomorrow, depending upon the opportunity. It is my understanding that Miss Culver is going to bring the Junior Literary Guild lady, Helen Ferris, into these parts, on or after the 21st. What with the coolness in the air, fires are in order and I found our Sepia Cinderella ranged before her fireplace, along with Jackie, Junior and Winnie Mae. It was interesting to me that when I mentioned Little Black Sambo that Jackie should glisten with that glow coming on anyone's face when discovering someone is talking about something that is comprehensible. I asked her if she knew the story. She said she had heard all about it, but had forgotten most of it, but could remember about the umbrella and how it ended. And so I left the manuscript, and I reckon before I got to the spillway, she was reading it to the assembled flock.

October 30, 1944

Helen Ferris was here with Miss Culver. I felt that her interest in Miss H.'s work was more in the nature of something interesting as a manifestation of art than as an expression of Art itself. It is my intention to keep in touch with her by correspondence following two or three different lines of endeavor which I know are close to her heart, and it is quite possible that once back on home ground, a quickened interest in items pertaining to this section may develop latently.

November 6, 1944

In regard to our little Sepia artist,—I went to see them on Saturday night and on Sunday night, but they must have been absent at the picture show both nights, for Sammy Balthazar had a movie both nights, and everybody I know attended,—two nights running. But as I understand it, the show played out on Sunday night, and so I shall take another crack down the road tonight,—and am sure Clemance will be enchanted to receive all the largesse stemming from your direction. The check, of course, came through safely, as did the package, and she will receive the former in full and the latter in part, for I think your suggestion that the presence of a paper shortage, plus the receipt of paper in small driblets, may tend to slow up her production a little and inspire her to greater quality. When I last saw her, she had quite an imposing stack of things to send. Among other things were some rather nice floral studies, and one or two portraits of "ladies looking at you." The latter whimsey seems to have been something which she just had to do, probably as a relaxation from too many rural scenes. As I saw them in lamp light they weren't particularly clear to me, but I shall leave it to you to determine what they show up as to the soul of little Mrs. H.

November 7, 1944

Election day for president. I called on our friends last night. It goes without saying that the girls were delighted to have the check. They cash it up at Ashely's so it doesn't go through the store here, and thus far everything appears to be rocking along nicely in that department. During my visit, we went over the last batch of paintings. It seemed to me that while many of them followed along familiar patterns there were a few which seemed to indicate a new departure. I would especially call your attention to the boy shucking corn. Although the light was rather indifferent, it somehow struck me that the angle or the medium or something was rather new. In a lesser way, I felt something of the same sensation in the case of the "Hospital picture," as Clemance calls it wherein the nurse is doing some-

thing with a baby over the bed of the mother of the child. Clemance painted out the presence of a lamp in the scene, saying that while Mary Frances had never been in a hospital, she had pointed out to her that they were bound to have a lamp in the place. There were quite a few good lines spoken, if you had only been present with your little note book. At the moment, I do not recall any of them exactly and of course it is the exactness which counts in such instances. With complete relaxation both ladies were laughing and talking quite freely, and among other things mentioned was this from Mary Frances: "Sometimes at night, Mama [Clemance] say she ain't goin' to paint nuthin' tonight, but before I can look around, she's done already painted two!" Whereupon Clemance giggled all over, leaned forward and rubbed her knee, and pointed out: "It looks like no matter how tired I is when it comes night, as soon as I light that lamp, a whole lot of things just start goin' 'cross my brain, and 'fore I knows it, I am getting them things down on paper."

December 4, 1944

You will be jealous when I tell you that I spent a couple of hours all alone on Sunday afternoon with Clemance. My primary purpose was to take down the little slip which had come to hand in Saturday's mail. She showed me a flock of pictures, but as several of them were still a little sticky,—it has been so humid of late,—we decided she should keep them until next week end when I shall pick them up and get them headed in your general direction. The most striking thing she has done is a concentration on the leaf department of some of her china-berry trees. I am under the impression that little Miss H. may not be up on her Bible to any great point of erudition. It seems to me that before she clashed with the mulatto color line in the local

Church, she went to the Catholic institution, and it is possible they didn't do much about acquainting their faithful with tales from the Old or New testament.

December 28, 1944

I saw Clemance in the store. She was looking as neat as a pin, and with some kind of new hair do,—I think it must be a new "swirlly" wig, or some such. She did look smart. She was buying a couple of cotton blankets, and asked me to point out to you that she was making this investment, as against the cold, with some of her Christmas money. Being on the scene, the clerk handed me the package of paints and brushes. I in turn handed them to her, and she was delighted. She says she has no more of the paper, as described in your letter.

January 20, 1945

The bundle for la belle Hunter came through safely, and she was enchanted. "Tell Mr. Pipes he sure done kept us'es from freezing this winter and that I thank him in the most high." She was really delighted.

February 5, 1945

It was good to have your letter on Saturday,—it had arrived earlier,—along with the package,—both of which Bill had saved for me at the store. Naturally, I hit out for your girl friend's house that night, and found her alone, and enchanted withal on receiving news from you, the eleven items and the paper. On Sunday afternoon, in a shower of rain, I paid her another visit, to see what had been cooking during the night,—and during my absence. You guessed it right,—she had labored before going to bed, and some of the items were quite nice. There is another decorative number of the type we like. There are also some charming floral pieces on the colored paper and one or two items with figures in them that are more or less in line with former compositions, but somehow,—to me,—seeming a bit balkan in their strong coloring. What with the dampness, they are still a little sticky, and I therefore left them on the walls, but will collect them later in the week and make a shipment about Friday or Saturday. Some of them I think you are going to like quite a lot.

February 9, 1945

Spring is in the air. Romance is budding. Because of these factors,—and others, I take the liberty to return your check herewith. The facts are these. Our girl friend, as you know, is at the moment a free soul,—what with the late Manuel Hunter having gone to his reward. One Yank Dudley, that black man who lives with Fougabou, is also a free soul,—and of all things, according to the darkies, the only virgin on Cane River. In his youth he married himself to the wine bottle in a big week end, and has remained faithful ever since,—sober from late Mondays until Saturday afternoons, and in the arms of his bottle from late Saturday until about noon on Monday. Since a little before Christmas, Yank has spent many evenings watching our girl friend paint. Those who know about such things say that Clemance needs somebody to cut her wood and do other chores. For his part, Yank needs someone to wash his clothes, act as seamstress for wear and tear developing over the week end, etc. Companionship knocks at the artist's portal, and in steps Yank. If ever there were an example of platonic friendship, in this remarkable example we find it. When asked,—but not by me,—

about an approaching nuptials, Clemance merely giggles. Yank says nothing. But that seems to be in the cards, and as Yank is even more of a Cane River number than Clemance, unquestionably the wedding will serve as an imperishable anchor for both parties to these shores. The present arrangement, too, permits the contracting parties to pool their respective incomes. For her part, it would seem to me that Clemance is quite satisfied with the checks of the usual denomination, plus what she acquires by her several bits of laundry she does for three or four families, which, added to her work in one of the camps, which I think she does mostly for the pleasure of "fooling around" white folks, sets her up very nicely financially. She has confided to me that she prefers to remain on Cane River, and that she needs but one thing to keep her happy at night when she is painting. She would ever so much like to have a radio,—a battery one, since she is always going to live away from town. If I may be so bold as to suggest it, I would think that in the event you should decide to maintain the usual stipend instead of increasing it, the excess might be conserved for the eventual purpose of a battery radio.

February 14, 1945

Your girl friend was enchanted with the package of clothing. So was Mary Frances,—but not with the clothes, which she ignored, once she laid sight of the two dolls, she snatched them up in a twinkling, and said that she didn't care about seeing anything else, and went over in the far corner of the room and began fondling them in a manner that would have made Santa Claus jealous. Jackie is writing the story of Wobley, Junior, or some such,—something about a duck which Clemance has illustrated to no great credit to herself, I think. She wants to send these illustrations with the story, and so they will come forward within a few days when Jackie has finished the text. The latter might be an interesting accompaniment, but, however that may be, the whole business will go forward shortly. I think I shall not wait for the other items, but send them along before Wobley, if possible. We talked about the Wake and Burial. She remembers how she did the Baptizing, and says she will try to do a Wake and Burial. I think the idea excellent,—to round out a life story, pictorially, in this series, and reckon we should have the finished product shortly. I have enlisted Clemance in our scouting plan regarding the property belonging to Regis' mamma. Clemance is going to contact the lady shortly with the statement that the sister in Alexandria wants to locate in Clemance's neighborhood and how much will the lady sell her strip of land for and when. Clemance is delighted to be of the party, and it seems to me such an approach would be excellent to secure a figure at a minimum. Then, too, it is nice to have Clemance giggling over the prospect, to be a part of the charade. In regard to the romance department, I might add that Yank appears to have established domestic contact. Judge Lindsey would pronounce it companionship marriage, and Negroes, without knowing about platonic friendship by name, say that Yank remains the only fifty year old virgin on Cane River. Clemance finds someone to help her empty her wash tubs, cut her wood etc. and so everything appears to be as each would have it, and Clemance pronounces herself at the moment as determined to remain in her present home.

February 28, 1945

Clemance came to see me yesterday. Having been under the weather, I haven't put my foot in the big road in ever so long. She tells me that she has completed the Baptizing and the

Burial,—or rather the Wake and Burial. From what she says, I conclude that it is a great pity we cannot have a transcription of her description of these masterpieces, for the word pictures are really grand.

March 8, 1945

I established contact with Clemance and we chatted much. I cannot recall how it was we hopped from one subject to another, but somehow we got around to the cutter of cards,—a very wise colored man, living off down Derry way, whom la belle noire has consulted from time to time. She told me quite frankly that she asked him about the future and that he told her the white folks she was tangled up with were really her best friends and advised her to stick with them through everything,—regardless. I'll bet the slick old fellow suspected hence came the six bits coming his way, as a result of her visit, but anyway that was music to her ears and of course confirmed what she has long since made up her mind to, and as it fits in nicely with our general agenda, I know you will concur in signifying a citation to the old rogue.

March 12, 1945

Miss Alberta Kinsey continues to paint, and to manifest interest in the Arts. When Clemance passed by the house the other day, Miss A. grabbed her off, took her to the Shop, and asked her to examine an impressionist painting she was doing. She asked Clemance where she would place the various colors, and lo! according to Miss A., Clemance indicated just the proper points, which greatly impressed Miss Alberta, and brought forth the observation from the Madam that Clemance was smarter than most people gave her credit. Clemance grinned at me when

Miss A. asked her if she did painting, and would she show her some. Clemance lied beautifully and declared that while she did paint from time to time, she always sent everything to her sister in Texas who sold the things for her. A day or two following, I thought I would make use of the lie and see what I could get by way of opinion out of Miss A. I admonished her to secrecy and confided to her that I sometimes did some painting and would show her a sample. What I had to point out to her was the one Clemance did in the Rousseau manner, the one framed in silver, formerly draped with the hat. Miss Alberta found it remarkable for me to have done such an excellent job, the perfection of the placing of colors, etc. She finds it so remarkably good that she wants to examine it further. White and green are the only things Clemance needs at the moment, she tells me.

March 13, 1945

I reckon you have received the paintings. I shall be interested to have your reaction. Obviously one would incline toward showing the Burial and the Baptizing in series form, since Clemance went in for panoramas. In the event you feel it better for her to try to compress the whole episode into one item, I shall make the suggestion to her. Regis' mama has not as yet come out of Texas, but Clemance is expecting her almost any old time, so her advent may be looked for any old time. Easter seems to draw lots of wayfaring mulattoes to Cane River at that time.

March 20, 1945

I am so glad you liked Clemance's latest efforts. Last night Alberta went into a vast discussion of the wonder of "my" silver framed masterpiece,—"such a marvelous sense of composition and color placement."

March 21, 1945

Carolyn Ramsey does articles and colored illustrations for Saturday Evening Post and special features for Life. She and Miss Culver arrived on Tuesday. This morning la Ramsey and I called on Clemance. We found her at her best. Her house was spotless, some swell numbers were on display, and Miss Ramsey loved every second of it. She proposes to return here within about six weeks. She will be delighted to "do" Clemance, and asked her if she would like to have her picture struck, especially one while she was painting before her fireplace, with several of her pieces of latest design hanging on the wall in the background. Clemance thought she would like that.

April 3, 1945

I took the black paper and the white paper to Clemance about nightfall. You will be glad to learn that she is her old self again, and it goes without saying that she was glad to have word from you. Mary Frances and Winnie Mae were playing about in the next room, and quite unmindful of the possibilities, I thought, what with the way they were sacheting the coal oil lamp around. Yank graced the sofa at Clemance's and added an occasional friendly albeit unimportant observation as to high water,—of which we are having much.

April 11, 1945

A lovely tent city has sprung up by the spillway, where Davis and Jackie live. Yesterday I called on the girl friend twice. In the afternoon I stood with her for an hour or so, while she hauled fish out of the spillway. We talked about you and other interesting people. Last night I dropped by the house with some turpentine, and viewed some of her latest creations. She appears to have done about a dozen flower prints on the black paper and she is going to finish out the collection with flower studies exclusively. The style is striking,—rather heavy for the most part, and illustrative of a new mood. There were two or three that seemed to me quite nice,—a bit heavy withal, but nicely balanced and I imagine altogether colorful. There were some,—perhaps four which seemed to be mostly heavy and that was about all, but possibly in the daylight they might appear more possessed of additional virtues. Off hand, however, I would say that about four, zinnias in bunches, seem to have great weight, both in feeling and excellence, although, as before opined, in a more titanic style, I thought, than some of her more delicate compositions. Out of the group there will be a goodly proportion that will be treasures.

April 22, 1945

It is impossible to get to Clemance's, what with water, hip high, pouring over the road at the spillway and a 30 foot complete wash out of the road beneath the surface of the waters. Being cut off as she is our artist friend ought to be casting off flower prints with abandon.

April 26, 1945

May I say that I saw a spick and span and nicely starched colored edition in the flesh of Madam Vigee Lebrun,—that is to say our own Clemance, who forded the mad waters still swirling over the spillway to get up here yesterday. She says she is doing alright and is painting madly.

May 2, 1945

What you really want to hear most is that I have visited little Miss Clemance and found her doing alright. She was up to her usual self, and seemingly somewhat satisfied with the fact that several of the refugees she has been housing have returned from whence they came a month ago,—off Little River way, I suppose. She explained that the presence of such a batch of folk made it impossible for her to do as much creative work as she would have liked, but she did show me some very pretty floral numbers she had done on the black paper. Only one of these carries a figure, a lady, somewhat suggestive of herself, arranging a huge vase of flowers. Somehow it seemed to me both fitting and original to have this item with the figure arranging the flowers as Illustration No. 1 for a collection of flower prints. It seems to me she said she had eight more sheets of paper to work on, and she herself suggested that she hold the others until she had completed the eighth, before sending them on to you. I concurred and last night I have no doubt the oil burned late in that cabin. She had quite a few little stories to tell me of the high water, including the fact that on Saturday night Yank got drunk and fell into the spillway, the muddy waters of that torrent passing over him. When he finally got home, covered with the red mud, she found that he looked like a pure "D" African. As for my uncertain vision, Yank had somehow always suggested that continental product a little, but to Clemance the coating of red mud seemed to put a seal on her husband or boy friend or whatever. You would have loved to hear her giggle and carry on.

May 3, 1945

You asked about the Vigee-Lebrun reference. She was the big portrait artist of France of the 18th century.

May 5, 1945

The two tubes of paint came through just before the spillway was swept away, so that our girl friend was fortified with that during the isolation period.

May 7, 1945

Bill's saloon just burned up. I am delighted, naturally, to have the copies of the newspaper, illustrating Clemance's picture. For the moment, I am not calling it to her attention. What with all the flood of late, and the presence in her neighborhood of white folks who sometimes worry her for pictures, I think, perhaps, it might be as well to hold her copy in camera for the moment, until,—at least, she is done with the black flower prints. I might even hold one of the copies until we can visit her together, just for the fun of seeing her reaction. She takes some things so casually and others with so much amusement, that it would really be fun to share it with you,—just to see what did happen,—if anything. When Yank was incorporated into the household, I nearly fell out with surprise, since it was about the last thing I had ever dreamed of, and what she may have to say about the thing in the newspaper, I cannot imagine. In regard to the flower prints on which she is currently engaged. I think I told you that she remarked, in showing me the one with the lady,—obviously herself, arranging the bouquet: "Maybe he would want to make a book out of this bunch with this one as the first picture." She thinks things so keenly sometimes, and other things she just isn't sufficiently interested to even toss it a glance. All in all, I think she is so swell, that I cannot wait to see what will happen, should Life do something about it. It is quite possible she might not even give it a second glance. One never can anticipate. I reached Clemance's house just about first dark, and found her at home, with Yank sitting along side the fireplace, and Mary Frances and Winnie Mae playing at house-keeping and Junior raising as much Hell as he could without foregoing the thumb from his mouth. Clemance was enchanted to have the box of paints,—the new box which arrived in Satur-day's mail. Clemance was pleased to receive the bags, which she explained, would make fine sheets, of which she had need at the moment. As for Mary Frances, she was captivated with the beads, both for the waist and the neck. The doll was a high point,—somehow welling up the infantile maternal complex, and balancing the maturity streak called forth by the beads. Mary Frances had to show all to Yank who thought them nice, and Clemance thought the doll was grand and she giggled and laughed, and Junior looked on a little wild-eyed, and backed off a little when Clemance tried to get him to kiss the white child. Clemance said she wasn't quite finished with the black sheets on which she is doing the flower prints. I told her not to hurry. Keeping her down to 60 miles an hour is difficult, and that was about the only way I could think of. I feel perfectly sure that as soon as I left the place, she got out her duffle and took a crack at the new tubes of paint.

May 16, 1945

A flock of flower prints on black paper go forward to you in this morning's mail. I saw youthful Miss Clemance yesterday afternoon about 1:30. I found her over the wash tub, standing on the ground with the tub on the south end of the front gallery, where a nice breeze was blowing and the pecans were casting a shade to cut the 95 degree thermometer reading. She appeared gay as a cricket, and had much by way of inquiry as to you and how much she hoped you would like some of the things she had been doing. Jackie was in the front yard, too, dressed up in a rather smart frock,—tan and pale yellow stripes, running horizontally about her svelt figure. I told Clemance that some people might come and ask about her painting and all, and that perhaps some of her pictures might be in a magazine. She said she didn't mind, and what did you and I think. I said I thought it would be nice and also it sure would set Miss Henry back. She giggled, and gave the sheet she was wringing a particularly vigorous twist, and we went inside to look over her collection. I think you will find some of them quite nice, in a decidedly heavy mood. You will note a couple of items on white paper, inspired by her neighbors during the flood, occupying Tent City, across the road from her. She pointed out one fling she made on black paper, recording that event. To my uncertain vision, it looked awfully African and wonderful. I hope to your own bright eyes it has something of the same effect. I think they are striking mani-festations of primitive art of a contemporary artist, unfettered by formalism, untutored save by a gift of God.

May 22, 1945

I was at the girl friend's again, thanks to the aid and comfort of a nice moon. Found her gay and industrious. She has tossed off a few new items,—one or two flower things, I think, and a couple of figures with frumpish lines,—one pushing a baby carriage, one nursing, and so on.

May 24, 1945

I am enchanted that you liked the latest doings of our girl friend so much. The fact that fire and water both figure in her latest efforts is good I think, since each type show a contemporary reaction to local events. The conflagration depicted the burning saloon.

May 31, 1945

Last night I put on my boots and went down the road. The road was dry, but the spillway is still in such an uproar that boots are a great help, what with the moon not rising until after midnight. I found our girl friend in fine form. It seems to me I haven't seen her so gay in spirits in years. She was delighted with the colored papers.

June 7, 1945

I saw our girl friend. She says, "Tell him I sure is glad to hear from him and about another week or so and we'll be a-fixin' to send him them flower prints." I found her in the road,—on the end of a string,—to the other end of which thrashed an overly energetic pig. She finally got him along side the old pecan tree where she tethered him for safe keeping,—his leg, the meanwhile, kicking as frantically as a stepped-up metronome. Inside the house, I looked over her latest efforts, done in the all-over pattern on the colored paper. I thought they seemed quite nice. I suppose the one appealing to me the most was a rather stiff spray of white zinnias, seemingly to have almost black stems. I believe they were on a powder blue paper, or at least so it seemed to me after stepping into the cool of her chamber from the glare of a brilliant sunshine outside. There was an added difference in

the accustomed lighting of the room, brought about by a quilt in its frames, which had been drawn up toward the ceiling, just beyond the top of my head. It was all very delightful and very Clemance.

June 16, 1945

I saw Clemance for a moment, and she said some pure "D" hill-billies had passed her house,—"all the mens and ladies barefeeted." Going to the spillway to fish, and that they wanted to buy some [pictures] and she wouldn't let them have any "no how."

June 21, 1945

I should say, that the Clemance work should be so grouped as to form a collection of folk painting, to be marketed first off in a group, as a high example of something or other. Once such a group was disposed of,—the whole illustrating the work of a rural and untutored genius, then her subsequent individual items could be marketed piece-meal.

June 22, 1945

It rained yesterday evening, and at sundown it cleared. Buckling or girding up my loins in rubber boots, I went down to see our girl friend, taking along with me some of the plunder which had recently come to hand, bearing the label: For the children. Both ladies were enchanted withal, and the neat little white sweater made Mary Frances pirouette about the place like a subdued whirling dervish. I added a dress to the assortment, also and that suited Clemance to a "T" and what with one thing and another, including à lanyap for Winnie Mae, everything in the house exuded delight and sable hued radiance. I brought back with me a number of examples of the latest endeavors. Some are quite good, some not, of course. There was much talk in the cabin about lampeels. It seems that Winnie Mae hoed one up in the cotton fields the other day. As you know they are quite harmless, but their appearance seemed to strike terror into everybody's heart. It was said that a man a long time back had been bitten by one and he never did get over it. I reckon the little "foots" is what introduces the terror.

June 29, 1945

Visited Clemance this afternoon about 2:00 and had a lovely sitting. She was looking quite cool, in spite of the excessive heat. She was barefooted, and with her it was all so nice and somehow of the true elegance that is part of the good earth, the sky and all the elemental things which are invariably in such good taste. About the 4th of July Clemance is going to get her pictures struck. Carolyn Ramsey is going to do the striking.

July 6, 1945

You will shortly receive a letter from Helen Baldwin, that is Mrs. Frank Baldwin of Waco, Texas. She wants to do everything she can to further us in our wish to put Clemance forward. She saw an item at Clemance's the other day when we were photographing the place she liked, and I think it a good investment to eventually have her take this home as a gift. It is one of Clemance's ladies.

July 7, 1945

The picture business goes on. Yesterday about 4:00 p.m. we ran down to see Clemance. Brother, who is King's little boy, about 6 years old, was with her, both grandmother and grandchild being about to undertake a fishing expedition. We got some fine shots, with Clemance just issuing from her front gate, fish pole on her shoulder, with Brother along side, carrying a bucket. The cabin formed a backdrop. With the gate white, and the supports of the gallery white, and the green wisteria vine against the gray wood of the house, a nice blue sky and a heap of big old clouds to round out the thing, I think the business is going to give the feeling of color, atmosphere and natural activity on the part of the participants, that will round out the other various phases of Clemance's day,—and to a very satisfying degree. Both Miss Ramsey and Mrs. Baldwin continue to express the greatest enthusiasm for Clemance's things. Mrs. B. asked Clemance if she would consider selling her a picture. Clemance was grand and said she left all that to you and me. I suggested we give the picture. Clemance beamed and said it sure would be nice. And when we said goodbye, everybody was happy all the way around.

July 9, 1945

The ladies departed yesterday (Sunday) afternoon. Plans going to be made for a Waco show.

July 14, 1945

Early in the evening—that is to say, at first dark,—I went to Clemance's. As she had lately received a generous assortment of clothes, the material for a red crepe dress went to Mary Frances, while the paint tubes went to Clemance. Divided into two parts, Clemance's little grandson, King's boy, Brother, got one portion of the candy, while Winnie Mae, along with Mary Frances, got the other part. I need not tell you that there was general frolicking among the young folks, while Clemance and Yank sat by and basked in the sunshine of the young folks' laughter. There was a nice moon but muggy heat and plenty of light bugs. Our girl friend has tossed off some figure pictures, and one or two of them are quite delicious. There is a set of two, wherein, in the first, a lady has hurt her footsie, and is having it attended by another lady. In the second picture, the footsie is obviously improving, and it is getting its final attention,—both scenes being the great out of doors, with gigantic flowers blooming merrily and a general setting of colorfulness that would be a treat to any sore eye. I hinted at the desirability of inserting a modest cloud as a backdrop for some of her paintings. In one or two she has undertaken since that time, terrific tornadoes have developed. I viewed them by lamplight and they were arresting.

July 18, 1945

I will turn to a prized personality to relate the latest gossip concerning the household of our girl friend, as reported on the "maternal peck go-round" by J. H. last night, when he spoke of local marital difficulties on the river. He said that Yank Dudley was complaining bitterly on Sunday that Clemance would not let him in the house, that she had been nice to him always until after he had brought home the groceries, but after that had refused to let him in the door. I suppose there were wet groceries involved, and little Miss Clemance got around to putting her foot down. Long before this writing, Yank has no doubt sobered up mightily and all is probably sweetness and light within the four walls of that little cabin they call home.

July 21, 1945

Carolyn Ramsey reports that she has forwarded the photographs to Life magazine that she made of Clemance. [Clemance] reports that she is about out of paper, and has a new batch of pictures to send shortly, some of them still being a little dampish. I examined them by lamplight. There were examples of the usual run of the mill, plus a few extraordinary ones, as inevitably the case. There is one in particular that I found especially elegant,— on black paper,—the figure of a lady moving between a big old flower on the right and a business, being a cross between a banana plant and a fleur-de-lis on the balancing side. The usual easily flowing lines in the skirt, plus the delightful harmony of blacks and grays, is especially appealing. I feel certain you are going to like them much.

July 25, 1945

There was a big old moon doing business last night, and long did I sit on our girl friend's gallery, talking with the greatest of satisfaction as to the general shape the Cane River pattern seems to be taking for the ensuing season, and of people we like, and how nice it is going to be when things get established.

July 26, 1945

I learn from Miss Ramsey that a couple of shots of Clemance's work has gone forward to Mrs. Baldwin for incorporation in next Sunday's paper, prior to the show in Waco. It sounds like publicity is operating. May the show do something in response.

August 1, 1945

About 7 p.m. I went to our friend's cabin. It was pleasant on her gallery, hot, of course, but a vague cool breeze stirring the leaves, and the general peace intensified by the velvety laughter of Junior, Winnie Mae, Mary Frances, and Brother,—King's little boy,—who were playing in the yard with White Child and Dora. Clemance and I talked on a whole flock of subjects and laughed constantly, she always collapsing forward, her forehead touching her palm on her knee. Yank sat on the other end of the gallery and added a quiet chuckle now and then. Clemance thought she could do something nice with the material and I assume she has already completed a bonnet by now. She says she could use some white paper and some green paint. She used a piece of black paper to toss off one item,—using an apple green paint as the major color, and as near as I could make out, it is quite lovely,—a depiction of cotton picking that I think is quite folk-lore-ish. You will like it eventually when you see it, I think. The heat remains excessive. I am writing several papers to be read at "So-say-shun" ["Association," an annual gathering to commemorate events of the past year].

August 6, 1945

I visited the girl friend Saturday night. It was hotter than a biscuit, and we sat long on her gallery and just talked local gossip endlessly, with nothing of especial interest, save the way she tossed off neatly original phrases, none of which seemed to stick in my mind. "So-say-shun" is to be August 15th. Baptizing is to be prior to that August 12th.

August 11, 1945

Baptizing this Sunday, August 12th. I went by King's house on Thursday night to share some Carnation with Clemance's grand-son, Brother, who figures with her in the fishing picture Miss Ramsey took. Brother ate too much Paris green a long time back, and his digestion never seems to have been quite right since.

August 18, 1945

"You tell 'em everything, 'cause everything is a crossin' my mind but I can't catch the words to say it all!" So said little Miss Clemance yesterday on receiving and unpacking her prize package. What with "So-say-shun" going full blast, I figured that there might be items in the shipment that would stand the lady in good stead and right off, so when it arrived yesterday morning, I immediately defied the hot, humid weather and flew down the road as fast as I could. Arriving about 11:00 a.m., my progress along the road must have been noticed by many, for no sooner had the girl friend started investigating the contents of the package than Jackie arrived, as did Winnie Mae, Mary Frances and Junior. King's wife, Renie, appeared a few minutes later with Beulah and somebody and Brother, to be followed immediately by Miss Willie, Jack and Ezra's mama, who lives next door. Not since Santa Claus made his first of innumerable rounds has there been quite so much excitement and glee. It would be difficult to say which one of the group was more impressed by the lavishness of the gifts, although I must say that Junior, thumb in mouth, was so fascinated by the black patent leather pocketbook that, hard as it is to imagine, he actually forgot his thumb for a little while. Before I knew it, the "Ho's" and "Ah's" had reached such a pitch that I was becoming suffocated. Accordingly, Brother, at the advanced age of six, and I thought we would walk a little piece, and so we took to the public road, heading in the general direction of Hyman's, until some of the excitement had died down. After the neighbors had departed, we returned to the cabin, finding Clemance busy as a bee, smoothing out one of the fine new frocks, preparatory to get fixed up for "So-say-shun." "Them folks sure did know me good," was her first remark. "Look how this fits like it was jus' made for me!" And so this Friday of Funerals at St. Matthews was bound to have been a great success, at least so far as Clemance was concerned and readily do I understand her sensation when remarking that I should "tell 'em everything, 'cause I can't say what's crossin' my mind."

October 6, 1945

I haven't written Lady Lake as yet, but intend to do so today. I am convinced that she will talk quite a bit about the glories of Cane River Art, if some local Club or Show place will undertake a display. Of late, I have had occasion to send a couple of notes to Mrs. Roosevelt, and in the event circumstances should intensify the trickle of correspondence to a flow, I think we might eventually send her a Cane River masterpiece along with a clipping from the Waco paper. It is premature to do so at the moment, I think, but a good opportunity might present itself later,—perhaps after the holidays. Eventually she might mention Clemance in her column, and that would be pleasant, too. I mention this possibility only as a possibility, but I think it pleasant to survey horizons now and then.

October 7, 1945

It was a moonless night with ample stars, and after dark I journeyed down to our girl friend's. Before reaching her cabin, I stood by the roadside for a while, listening to the raucous sound of some curious music, issuing forth from the phonograph which I gave her a week or so back. There was something about the non-descript racket that was as weird as St. Elmo's fire flitting unpredictably above an uncertain marshland. On the gallery our girl friend was sitting in a straightback chair, silhouette etched by the kerosene lamp from within the house. Mary Frances and Winnie Mae frolicked about with Junior. King sat on the steps, puffing a cigarette. Yank was stretched out full length on the gallery, in the shadows. Inside, Jackie was twisting the old music box for all it was worth,—and in a way that wasn't much, as measured by some folkses,—but priceless as judged by our standards. I joined the group. The music and children toned down a little, but not much. Eventually Jackie took the children and went over to King's house with him. Our girl friend and I,—Yank snoring softly,—sat and reminisced mostly talking about the time when Emanuel was sick and "Mr. Pipes and you" used to come down and consolate him. Strangely enough there was a dual thread running through the thing,—a certain nostalgia and intermittent giggles, that made a most delicious and heady brew for souls such as hers and yours and mine. And I slipped her the check and she and I then went inside to examine her latest handiwork. Some of it is quite average. There is one with a new treatment, that you are going to like. It is a lady in bed, fanning herself, and another lady at the foot of the bed, handing her a cup of something or other. The figures aren't important, however,—it's the treatment of the drapery or sidewalls of the interior,—or the sheer decoration,—or whatever I couldn't make it out very distinctly, but the impression was definite and unmistakably individualistic and distinctive.

October 17, 1945

What with a big moon waxing this week, I have twice

journeyed down to see our girl friend, but each time there appeared to be no light in the place and so I have passed slap by, assuming that these chill days in the cotton patch may have inclined our girl friend to fold up early. But I know perfectly well that had I made another go-round along about midnight or perhaps 2:00 a.m., I would see a light streaming through the cracks in the cabin door and were I to peer in, I should see her wielding brushes for all they are worth. The other day when I saw Mary Frances I asked her if she and Clemance were resting a bit now that they were snowed under with cotton. Mary Frances giggled and said that almost every night she would ask Clemance if she intended painting, and the answer would be negative,— and that every time, after the elder of the two had jumped into the bed, she would "worry around" for a little while, and then bolt out from under the covers and lighting the lamp, start in to mark something down.

October 18, 1945

Mary Frances brought Brother by to see me, and after we had toasted our footsies before the fire for half an hour, Mary Frances went back to her cotton-picking, and Brother had his first go-round with me. Yesterday on the store gallery I saw a figure that looked ever so much like one million dollars. Of course, as you have already guessed, it was our girl friend. She had on an outfit that some of us sometime or other provided,— with yellow the basic color, with a value equal to that of olive,— were an olive yellow instead of green. Her headgear was of the same material, and regal was the word for Clemmy. I told her that I had been sauntering by her house for a couple of nights in vain hope of catching a ray of lamplight through a chink in the door. Her first utterance convinced me that her statement was

only too true. She really has quite a cold, but cold or no cold, she looked simply elegant. She tells me that she will have some more pictures to send this weekend, and I shall get down,— sometime or other,—to get them, but I am not sure just when. Sick as she is, she continues to do the laundry, and when the "misery" in her back gets her down in the cotton rows, she drops her sack, and grabs a fish pole and Yank and all dine on fine specimens from the river that would make Isaac Walton green with jealousy.

October 30, 1945

I am sending an imposing collection of our girl friend's latest masterpieces. I think the average is pretty good,—especially in view of all the picking of cotton, washing of clothes, scrapping of pecans, making of gardens, cooking of meals, making over of garments, running of a household, etc. which have just naturally had claims on the whole business. I think I mentioned the interesting composition, the lady in bed fanning herself with another lady standing at the foot of the bed doing something or other. I thought the drapery or background or whatever of this composition quite interesting. Some of the compositions, it seems to me are a little dark,—possibly a little muddy. I am under the impression that had these been done in daylight, they might have been a little more satisfactory. I think you will agree with me that one or two of the ladies,—a single figure in a composition or sometimes as two figures, are quite elegant. The military caps on one set of ladies is a new note, and there is one rather busy picture with lots of small figures scattered around on the ground, which our girl friend says she calls doll's house. In view of all the time and energy put upon our girl friend during the recent weeks, I think this collection quite good. I presume that when the pecans and cotton are over and done with, she may find time to do a bit of daylight painting, and it will be interesting to see how much compositions contrast in brilliancy of color with those contrived by the light of the lamp.

November 8, 1945

To get back to the masterpieces, I thought the picture of the religious flavor was quite interesting from its angle of newness of approach. I have a feeling she is anxious to strike off another in that vein, and I shall be looking for the two packages you mentioned as being on the way. Our girl friend's heart is going to be glad, and I am sure mine is too. I visited Clemance. She was much elated at both items I presented to her in your behalf. She asked me most especially to say how much she appreciated the smaller slip, since she had been having trouble with her toofies and had made two trips to town lately, and that the slip will help her along good in securing her new "Wrack." But knowing Clemance as you do, you may be quite sure that a trip to the dentist would scarcely cover all her activities, and Lo! there was a couple of new masterpieces, each depicting her impression of the statue of "The Good Darkie." Pointing to the first she had done, she explained that she hadn't had a very good look on her first trip. There was some curious way she had arranged the hat which the old man is doffing,—as I recall, I think she had the crown of the derby up in the air, rather than toward the ground, which produces a very curious impression, as well you might imagine, should you attempt to tip your hat in such a manner so that the top of the hat would be up rather than down. Well,

anyhow, it seems that on her second go-round, she had glimpsed the thing speedily but to advantage, and there the second go at the thing was, and it looked pretty good.

November 9, 1945

Congratulations on the Rosenwald business in behalf of Clemance. As soon as the blanks arrive we shall get them fixed up.

November 15, 1945

It goes without saying that I was so pleased to read of the telegram both from and to our Fort Worth acquaintants. I have a feeling that la Lake is already sharpening up her goose quill, to write something momentous about the Art of Clemance Hunter, for I think she loved to air her knowledge of that branch of the arts, and if she will convince herself that she has discovered another Rosa Bonheur or some such, then I think the local publications in the Fort Worth area will fairly glow with her praises of her Cane River mystery woman. I saw our girl friend yesterday, and we had quite a chat together. She had recently acquired from the Madam a most curious old chromo, in the form of a frame,—about three feet long and perhaps 18 inches wide,—much filagree, painted white, but considerably dowdy and forgotten Gay 90 in appearance. I am just wondering what she will stir up to suit that frame. You may be sure that it will turn out to be something you can at least hang your hat on.

Commentary

CRITICAL COMMENT ON Clementine Hunter's art has been largely favorable over the years, though she has not been without her detractors. Certainly her childlike, often awkward style can be disconcerting to those who would disallow primitive art or folk art as a serious artistic enterprise. But that is a problem that has plagued many such artists over the years.

While some critics and art historians are inclined to classify her as a *primitive* artist, more seem to prefer to call her a *folk* artist. (Indeed she has been pointed to as one of America's foremost primitive painters on the one hand, and as one of the preeminent folk artists of the twentieth century on the other.) She has also been categorized as a *naive* painter and as a *memory* painter. In one way or another, all seem to apply.

Art historians, as a rule, take the position that folk art is not naive and simple. They insist that because the artist does not articulate the history of his or her art does not mean it lacks intelligence. And, they say, while technique may lag, or may even be consciously ignored, a powerful "flash of the spirit" is always evident in the best.

The spirit of Hunter's art is first noticed in her evocative use of color, as her earliest critics pointed out. Carter Stevens, an art critic for the *New Orleans Item*, described her art as "vivid and joyous" in his review of a collection which appeared in the 1949 New Orleans Arts and Crafts Show. He wrote:

> She is a primitive painter true and simple with a wonderful flare for colors and an intuitive grasp of composition. She is a painter born, never had a lesson in her life. . . .
>
> Clementine Hunter's painting of a bouquet of flowers is as vivid and joyous as sun-up on a beautiful day when one is 16 years old, and her "Sunday Afternoon" is enchanting folklore on canvas. Life must be fun on Cane River.

Edward J. Steichen, a giant in the world of photography, echoed Stevens' opinion of Hunter art in a 1956 article for *Holiday* magazine. Steichen was noted for his adventurous experiments with color and for his fondness for breaking conventions. Perhaps he saw in Hunter a little of himself. In illustrating what he called "the living joy of pictures," he chose a Hunter painting and said:

> The painter's imagination, unchecked by the conventions and limits of earlier periods of art, today can range in total freedom, exuberantly choosing its own subjects, its brilliant colors and incredibly variegated techniques . . . [as illustrated in] the subtle and compelling work of . . . Clementine Hunter, a Negro from Louisiana.

Even before her first public notices, Hunter was receiving critical support from notables in the art world. In the early 1940s, during a visit to Melrose Plantation, American writer Alexander Woollcott viewed some of her paintings and was impressed. He found her use of color not only arresting but saw it as a source of inspiration for "confused" contemporary artists, many of whom he felt couldn't communicate with anyone other than themselves. In a statement to Melrose curator François Mignon, Woollcott said:

> I like Clemence's paintings. Too long has contemporary American Art been floundering around blindly. There is something so original, so colorful and convincing in them that I am convinced they may prove to be the seeing-eye that may lead many a confused artist with more formal training back on the right road to a self expression that others than the artist can comprehend.

A prominent woman of letters, Alice B. Toklas, was likewise a Hunter enthusiast. She found something powerfully civilized in her primitive style and, like Woollcott, saw the artist's colorful canvases as a source of inspiration for contemporary artists. She wrote in a 1957 letter to Mignon:

> It was delightful to receive your letter yesterday morning and the most complete surprise to receive by the next postal delivery Clementine Hunter's astonishing painting. . . . I wrote [her] a few lines to tell her how much her painting impressed me. It is really not at all primitive. It is very civilized—as Gertrude Stein said of the African wood carvings that influenced Matisse and particularly Picasso, almost fifty years ago.

By the mid-1970s, Hunter was well established as a folk artist, and critics had begun to look beyond her explosive colors to the soul of her art. More and more attention was being given to her subject matter—its emotional as well as historical force. And as her role as a cultural transfer agent became recognized and understood, the significance of her work grew.

In her 1975 book, *Contemporary American Folk Artists*, Elinor Horwitz described for folk art cognoscenti Hunter's growing popularity and the appeal of her art. She wrote:

> Clementine Hunter, the elderly illiterate black servant who spent almost seventy-five years . . . at Melrose Plantation, has become more famous than the cultivated guests who spoke of Rodin and Michelangelo at the dinner table. . . . Her paintings are naive in execution, joyous, spontaneous, radiant with color. They depict all aspects of life in the rural South. . . . Clementine Hunter paints only happy memories.

Meanwhile, Allen Rankin, in a 1975 article for *Reader's Digest*, explained it to the masses:

> Why all the excitement about her work? In America there

are thousands of good folk artists. . . . Primarily, say her fans, because her pictures present a nostalgic, authentic and charming view of that fast-vanishing pageant, Negro life on the Southern plantation. They see in [her] exuberant canvases a record of a host of black people who, though luckless in the time and place of their existence, nevertheless made meaningful, then joyous, use of their lives.

And in 1979, Robert Bishop, the director of the American Museum of Folk Art in New York, acknowledged the artist's prominence and importance in his book, *Folk Painters of America.* He wrote:

Clementine Hunter of Melrose Plantation . . . is perhaps the most celebrated of all Southern contemporary painters. Hunter knows well the black life that she so touchingly portrays, for as an illiterate black servant she spent over sixty-five years in the fields and as kitchen help at Melrose. It was not until her late sixties* that Clementine Hunter began to paint her radiant naive pictures that depict life and death in a rural Southern setting.

In a later interview Bishop said, "I think she's wonderful. She's an important artist. Her work is uneven, but every artist's work is uneven. Not every Rembrandt is a wonderful Rembrandt."

By 1980, Hunter was established as one of the matriarchs of contemporary folk art. "The continuous line of self-taught female folk painters, beginning in the 18th century, continues today with such famous folk artists as Grandma Moses, Clara Robertson, and the black folk artist Clementine Hunter," wrote Charlotte S. Rubinstein in her 1982 book, *American Women Artists.*

Actually, Hunter began painting in her mid-fifties.

At the same time, her art was being challenged by some critics. There were those who had been watching her develop for many years and who, like Bishop, had detected an unevenness in her work. The unevenness was more troubling for some than for others.

In a 1981 review of a gallery showing in New Orleans, art critic Roger Green, writing for the *Times Picayune/States Item,* expressed his concern:

Too many of Hunter's paintings . . . —particularly views of cotton wagons and, unhappily, all of her pictures with religious themes—are simply crude in a manner that fails to strike responsive emotional or intellectual chords in the viewer. These paintings are artless in the clumsy, unrewarding, negative sense of the term.

One must, of course, consider the genuine feeling that underlies Hunter's paintings, and the unselfish motives that seem to have impelled many of the promoters of her art. But these secondary considerations are not, from the point of view of quality in art, enough.

Green's criticism found support from other critics who suggested that Hunter's art was, at times, perfunctory and perhaps manufactured merely for commercial purposes. At the worst, it was called decorative art.

The artist never denied that she turned out some paintings on demand, especially in her later years, in order to generate income. Having painted several thousand pictures, many of them repetitions of popular scenes, it is evident that hers was not a totally improvident art. And, only a few critics found serious fault with this "commercialization," most apparently willing to accept it as a small impurity in an otherwise honest art. Most, too, were able to concede that the artist's "genuine feelings" were indeed central to her art.

"She painted because she wanted to," said Sterling Cook, Curator Emeritus at the Miami University Art Museum in Oxford, Ohio. "She didn't care if anybody wanted them and that's what makes them good.

"There are all sorts of folk artists—black and white—but the really good ones have gotten on in life and have some perspective on life. They have a certain naive charm, are very sincere and not very contrived."

It was in her earliest works that critics began to find the definitive Hunter, and most have said that these will stand the test of time. Mimi Read, a *Times Picayune/States Item* writer, described the stability of these early pieces in a 1985 article for that newspaper. She wrote:

> Hunter's early paintings are visions from her gut and heart. They are naive in execution, joyous in spirit and full of imagination. Red longjohns pinned to clotheslines waltz theatrically in the breeze. Giant chickens pull wagonloads full of loose, frothy cotton. Even her funeral scenes have a festive air—the corpse rests in a coffin as gay as a birthday cake, the women sport confectionery bonnets and the sky is a clean sweep of baby blue.

And Kenneth C. Danforth wrote for National Geographic in 1987:

> She grasps anything within reach—window shades, shoe boxes, paper sacks, snuff bottles—and floods it with bright colors until an exuberant narrative unfolds. . . . She paints entirely from memory.

Indeed, memory seems to have been the only reliable source of her art. Any effort to work from a model, from a present reality, always ended in disappointment and even pain. She had to remember it in order to paint it.

What she remembered was a simple, predictable, repetitive life. Her art reflects that. What she remembered was a symmetrical, uncomplicated, and unsophisticated life. And her art reflects that. What she remembered was a kind of brilliant, colorful joy, in life and in death. If there is fault in that, then that is the fault in her art.

Her art could hardly be more straightforward. "She simply picks up a brush and puts down remembered scenes from Southern life," wrote *Los Angeles Times* art critic Suzanne Muchnic in August 1986. "There's little subtlety and sophistication in her work. She often applies pigment straight from the tube and deals with perspective by painting horizontal stripes of action, but she has a sure sense of design and an indomitable spirit.

"Though some critics and art historians have tried to account for the 'African influence' in her work or line it up with Haitian and Coptic art, Hunter will have none of it. She's nothing more nor less than an unpretentious, natural artist. She's aware of her fame but apparently impervious to the art world's need to classify her personal expression."

Hunter almost refuses to be classified. She did not consider herself an artist, nor, as some have said, a genius. If anything, she considered herself merely as one who lived a life—largely a happy one. What happened on her canvases, she considered a miracle of God and nothing of her own doing.

The art of living is what Hunter paintings have been all about, suggests New Orleans art critic Juliana Harris-Livingston. And while she took the simplest approach, perhaps that has been the best. Less is sometimes more, as the critic noted: "Perhaps because her miracles are simple ones, accessible to all, she moves her audience beyond the obvious primitivism and into the deeper poignancy of life itself."

APPENDIX

Permanent Collections

Northwestern State University, Natchitoches, La.

Louisiana State University, Baton Rouge, La.

High Museum, Atlanta, Ga.

Dallas Museum of Fine Arts, Dallas, Tex.

New Orleans Museum of Art, New Orleans, La.

Radcliffe College, Cambridge, Mass.

Vassar College, Poughkeepsie, N.Y.

New York Historical Association, New York City

Capital Children's Museum, Washington, D.C.

J. Broussard Collection, Louisiana Division of the Arts, Baton Rouge, La.

Illinois State University, Normal, Ill.

Fisk University, Nashville, Tenn.

University of Texas at Arlington

Birmingham Museum of Art, Birmingham, Ala.

Tulane Medical Center, New Orleans, La.

Louisiana Arts and Science Center, Baton Rouge, La.

Touro Infirmary, New Orleans, La.

Trafton Academy, Baton Rouge, La.

African House, Melrose Plantation, Natchitoches, La.

Cabildo, New Orleans, La.

Old State Capitol Gallery, Baton Rouge, La.

Rural Life Museum, Baton Rouge, La.

Shows and Exhibits

Adams U.S.O. by the Junior Twentieth Century Club, Brownwood, Tex., November 1945

New Orleans Arts and Crafts Show, New Orleans, La., 1949

New Orleans Museum of Art, New Orleans, La., 1952

The Saturday Gallery, St. Louis, Mo., 1954

*"Clementine Hunter: Primitive Painter," Northwestern State University, Natchitoches, La., May 1955

Delgado Museum, New Orleans, La., May 1955

Dillard University, New Orleans, La., February 1968

*"Clementine Hunter," Louisiana State University, Baton Rouge, La., 1970

*Grambling College, Grambling, La., October 1970

La Jolla Museum of Contemporary Art, San Diego, Calif., 1970

"Louisiana Folk Paintings," Museum of American Folk Art, New York City, September–November 1973

Louisiana Arts and Science Center, Baton Rouge, La., December 1973–January 1974

*Fisk University, Nashville, Tenn., 1974

*Security National Bank, Alexandria, La., 1974

*Bank of New Orleans, New Orleans, La., February 11–March 1, 1974

*Louisiana Bank and Trust Company, Shreveport, La., 1975

Concordia Art and Garden Festival, Ferriday, La., May 3, 1975

*"Clementine Hunter Exhibit," The Barnwell Center, Shreveport, La., August–September 1975

*"Clementine Hunter Exhibit," Sister's Gallery, Memphis, Tenn., May 1976

Los Angeles County Museum of Art, Los Angeles, Calif., 1976

"Two Centuries of Black American Art," Los Angeles County Museum of Art, Los Angeles, Calif., September 30–November 21, 1976 (traveling exhibit):
    Brooklyn Museum, Brooklyn, N.Y., June 1977

*Lauren Rogers Library and Museum of Art, Hattiesburg, Miss., May 1977

"The Afro American Tradition in the Decorative Arts," Cleveland Museum of Art, Cleveland, Ohio, February 1–April 2, 1978 (traveling exhibit):

    Milwaukee Art Center, Milwaukee, Wis., May 4–July 2, 1978

    Birmingham Museum of Art, Birmingham, Ala., September 10–November 5, 1978

    Museum of Fine Arts, Boston, Mass., December 5, 1978–January 11, 1979

    St. Louis Art Museum, St Louis, Mo., March 22–May 13, 1979

    Henry Gallery, University of Washington, Seattle, Wash., June 21–September 2, 1979

    Smithsonian Institution, Washington, D.C., Fall 1979

"Black Artists/South," Huntsville Museum of Art, Huntsville, Ala., 1979

*Exchange Bank and Trust Company, Natchitoches, La., 1979

"Y'all Come—Louisiana Native/Folk Art," Anderson-Hopkins Gallery, Washington, D.C., February 13–April 6, 1979

*"A Black Woman on the Move," Barksdale Air Force Base Library, Barksdale Air Force Base, La., February 1980

*University of Texas at Arlington, February–March 1980

"Southern Works on Paper, 1900–1950," Montgomery Museum of Fine Arts, Montgomery, Ala., 1981

*Grambling College, Grambling, La., March 1981

*"Primitive Paintings by Clementine Hunter," Gasperi Folk Art Gallery, New Orleans, La., March 1981

"Forever Free: An Exhibit of Art by African-American Women, 1862–1980," Illinois State University, Normal, Ill., January 1981 (traveling exhibit):

    Joslyn Art Museum, Omaha, Nebr., March–April 1981

    Montgomery Museum of Fine Arts, Montgomery, Ala., June–July 1981

    Gibbes Art Gallery, Charleston, S.C., September–October 1981

    The Art Gallery, University of Maryland, College Park, Md., October–December 1981

    Indianapolis Museum of Art, Indianapolis, Ind., January–February 1982

Centenary College, Shreveport, La., 1982

*"Clementine Hunter," Gilley's Gallery, Baton Rouge, La., 1982

"Where Now, Black Man," University of Texas at Arlington, February 1982

"What It Is: Black American Folk Art from the Collection of Regenia Perry," Anderson Gallery, Virginia Commonwealth University, Richmond, Va., October 6–27, 1982

"Black Artist—The Woman's Touch," University of Texas at Arlington, February 1983

"A Shifting Wind: Views of American Folk Art," Fennimore House Gallery, New York State Historical Association, Cooperstown, N.Y., 1983–84

Louisiana Folklife Exhibit, World's Fair, New Orleans, La., 1984

*"The Schoephoerster Collection: Paintings by Clementine Hunter," St. Olaf College, Northfield, Minn., January 1984

*Louisiana State University at Shreveport, February 1984

*Bossier Bank and Trust Company, Bossier City, La., May 1984

*Louisiana Arts and Science Center, Baton Rouge, La., October 1984

"Black Women Artists: Achievements Against the Odds," Anacostia Neighborhood Museum, Smithsonian Institution, Washington, D.C., October 1984

"American Art in Louisiana Private Collections, 1870–1970," Louisiana Arts and Science Center, Riverside Gallery, Baton Rouge, La., February 1985

*"Clementine Hunter," Dillard University, New Orleans, La., February 1985

City National Bank, Baton Rouge, La., February 14–March 14, 1985

"Twentieth Century American Folk Art," deSaisset Museum, University of Santa Clara, Santa Clara, Calif., January 12–March 17, 1985

*"A Centennial Salute to Clementine Hunter," New Orleans Museum of Art, New Orleans, La., February 23–April 28, 1985

"Clementine Hunter," California Afro-American Museum, Los Angeles, Calif., August 1986

"Two Black Folk Artists," Miami University Art Museum, Oxford, Ohio, January 10–March 15, 1987

*"Clementine Hunter Collection on Exhibit," South Arkansas Art Center, El Dorado, Ark., April 3–30, 1987

*"Clementine Hunter: 40 Years of Painting," Alexandria Museum Visual Art Center, Alexandria, La., May 2–June 30, 1987

"Clementine Hunter," International Folk Art Festival, Sailor's Valentine Gallery, Nantucket, Mass., July 17–23, 1987

*One-woman shows or exhibits

Selected Bibliography

Primary Sources

Archives and Special Collections, Cammie G. Henry Research Center, Eugene P. Watson Memorial Library, Northwestern State University of Louisiana, Natchitoches, La. (James Register Collection, François Mignon Collection, Melrose Collection, Thomas N. Whitehead Collection.)

Archives of St. John the Baptist Church, Cloutierville, La.

Archives of the Chapel of St. Augustine, Isle Breville, Natchitoches Parish, La.

Bailey, Mildred H. "Clementine Hunter." *Four Women of Cane River—Their Contributions to the Cultural Life of the Area.* Natchitoches, La.: Natchitoches Parish Library, 1980.

Black Women Oral History Project. Interview with Clementine Hunter, November 29, 1979. Cambridge, Mass.: Schlesinger Library, Radcliffe College, 1980.

Censuses of Natchitoches Parish, 1900 and 1910.

Clerk of Court's Offices, Natchitoches Parish Courthouse, Natchitoches, La.

Collection of Mildred Hart Bailey, Natchitoches, La.

Interviews with Clementine Hunter by the biographer, 1987.

Interviews with Thomas N. Whitehead and Mildred Hart Bailey by the biographer, 1987.

Mignon, François. *Plantation Memo: Plantation Life in Louisiana, 1950–70, and Other Matters*; edited with introduction by Ora Garland Williams. Baton Rouge, La.: Claitor's Publishing Division, 1972.

Mills, Gary B. and Elizabeth. *Melrose*. Natchitoches, La. Association for the Preservation of Historic Natchitoches, 1973.

Secondary Sources

Stevens, Carter. "DiFranco Painting Tops at Art Exhibit." *New Orleans Item*, August 18, 1949.

Willard, Charlotte. "Innocence Regained." *Look*, June 16, 1953, pp. 103–5.

"Melrose Artist to Have Delgado Museum Exhibit." *Natchitoches Times*, April 29, 1955.

McDonald, Margaret. "Clementine the Painter." *Shreveport Times*, May 8, 1955.

Mignon, François and Hunter, Clementine. *Melrose Plantation Cookbook*. Natchitoches, La.: Baker Printing, 1956.

Steichen, Edward J. "The Living Joy of Pictures." *Holiday*, March 1956, pp. 112, 114–16.

Williams, Ora G. "Clementine Hunter: Primitive Artist of Louisiana." *Sunday Advocate*, Baton Rouge, La., September 26, 1965.

Eakin, Sue. "A Louisiana Profile: François Mignon." *Louisiana Heritage*, Fall 1968, pp. 33–34, 46.

Miller, Herschel. "Clementine Hunter—American Primitive." *New Orleans*, December 1968, pp. 6–11 and the cover.

Morris, Steven. "The Primitive Art of Clementine Hunter." *Ebony*, May 1969, pp. 144–48.

Register, James. *The Joyous Coast*. Illustrations by Clementine Hunter. Shreveport, La.: The Mid-South Press, 1971.

Dowdy, Verdis. "The Fame of Clementine's Primitives." *Centre Magazine*, Alexandria, La., 1972.

Register, James. "Clementine Hunter and the World Around Us." *Natchitoches Times*, December 17, 1972.

Louisiana Folk Paintings. New York: Museum of American Folk Art, 1973. (Catalogue)

Register, James. "Artist Clementine Hunter—The Magic Touch." *Alexandria Daily Town Talk*, February 19, 1973.

Gibson, Mary. "The Primitive Painter from Melrose Plantation." *Family Circle*, August 1973, p. 46.

Mignon, François. "Hunter Show in Manhattan." Cane River Memo in *Natchitoches Times*, October 14, 1973.

Hemphill, Herbert W., Jr., and Weissman, Julia. *Twentieth-Century American Folk Art and Artists*. New York: E. P. Dutton, 1974.

Register, James. "Those Things Make My Head Sweat." *Natchitoches Times*, February 28, 1974.

Horwitz, Elinor Lander. *Contemporary American Folk Artists*. Philadelphia: J. B. Lippincott, 1975.

King, Elaine. "Clementine Hunter, Artist, Found on a Talkative Day." *Shreveport Times*, February 2, 1975.

Register, James. "'Your Sky is Too Low,' Says Clementine Hunter." *Natchitoches Times*, February 6, 1975.

Smith, Laurie. "Clementine Hunter Still Painting." *State Times*, Baton Rouge, La., July 9, 1975.

Rankin, Allen. "The Hidden Genius of Melrose Plantation." *Reader's Digest*, December 1975, pp. 118–22.

Driskel, David C. *Two Centuries of Black American Art*. New York: Alfred A. Knopf, 1976.

1976 UNICEF Engagement Calendar. New York: United Nations, 1976.

"Making Her Mark." *Mid-South Magazine* in *Commercial Appeal*, Memphis, Tenn., April 11, 1976.

Northrop, Gary. "Living With Art—Clementine Hunter: First Look for Memphis." *Commercial Appeal*, Memphis, Tenn., May 23, 1976.

"Hidden Genius of Melrose Plantation." *Reader's Digest*, Japanese Edition, 1977, pp. 52–57.

Burnett, W. C., Jr. "Black Art Evolves." *Atlanta Journal and Constitution*, January 9, 1977.

"Clementine Hunter: The Black Grandma Moses." *Fleur de Lis* (Tabloid), April–May 1977.

"Clementine is Leaving Melrose." *Natchitoches Times*, June 2, 1977.

Mignon, François. "More Rue Christine Letters." Plantation Memo in *Shreveport Times*, September 11, 1977.

Vlach, John Michael. *The Afro-American Tradition in Decorative Arts.* Cleveland, Ohio: Cleveland Museum of Art, 1978.

Mignon, François. "Artist's Fame Spreads to Asia, Japan." Plantation Memo in *Shreveport Times*, January 8, 1978.

"Hunter House is Moved." *Natchitoches Times*, April 6, 1978.

Allen, Helen. "Clementine Hunter Continues Melrose Tradition." *Monroe Morning World*, April 30, 1978.

Register, James. "Clementine—I Just Likes to Paint." *Natchitoches Times*, June 4, 1978.

Register, James. "Cane River Artist 'Just a Painter.'" *Alexandria Daily Town Talk*, June 11, 1978.

Knight, Margaret R. "She Still Marks Pictures." *Sunday Advocate*, Baton Rouge, La., August 27, 1978.

"Heroics of Louisiana Women Noted." *Morning Advocate*, Baton Rouge, La., December 10, 1978.

Bishop, Robert. *Folk Painters of America.* New York: E. P. Dutton, 1979.

Dewhurst, C. Kurt, MacDowell, Betty, and MacDowell, Marsha. *Artists in Aprons.* New York: E. P. Dutton, 1979.

Hudson, Ralph M. *Black Artists/South.* Huntsville, Ala.: Huntsville Museum of Art, 1979.

Y'all Come. Washington, D.C.: Anderson-Hopkins Gallery, 1979. (Catalogue)

Mignon, François. "Washington Exhibit of Louisiana Art." Cane River Memo in *Natchitoches Times*, May 1979.

Register, James. "Fate Decreed that Clementine Hunter Would Become Artist She is Today." *Natchitoches Times*, June 3, 1979.

Flora, Doris P. "Historic Black Artists/South Exhibit Reflects 200 Years of Ethnic Heritage in America." *Art Voices South*, July/August 1979, pp. 21–22.

"Exhibits Span Primitive, Complex." *UTA Newsprint*, University of Texas at Arlington, February 1980.

Forever Free: An Exhibit of Art by African-American Women, 1862–1980. Normal, Ill.: Illinois State University, 1980. (Catalogue)

Kutner, Janet. "Exhibition Spotlights American Folk Artist." *Dallas Morning News*, March 9, 1980.

"Hunter Paintings Now on Exhibit." Arts in *UTA Shorthorn*, University of Texas at Arlington, June 1980.

"Two Clementine Hunter Works Donated to Library." *UTA News and Development*, University of Texas at Arlington, June 1980.

Cox, Richard. *Southern Works on Paper, 1900–1950.* Atlanta, Ga.: Southern Arts Federation, 1981. (Catalogue)

Green, Roger. "Clementine Hunter: Naivete Is Not Enough." World of Art in *Times Picayune*, March 6, 1981.

Martin, Margaret. "At 96, She Paints What She Knows." *Shreveport Times*, March 29, 1981.

"A Plantation Carved From Legend." *Southern Living*, April 1981, pp. 2sw–8sw.

Harris-Livingston, Juliana. "Hunter's Folk Art: Rockmore's Invention." *Gambit*, New Orleans, La., April 4, 1981.

Ryan, Robert and Ryan, Yvonne. "Clementine Hunter." *Louisiana Life*, September/October 1981, pp. 32–42.

Bailey, Mildred Hart. "Painted Memories of a Slave's Daughter." *Modern Maturity*, October–November 1981, pp. 42–44.

Hunt, Charles. "View From the Other Castle." *Artspectrum*, Louisiana Division of the Arts and Louisiana State Arts Council, December 1981, p. 16.

Perry, Regenia. *What It Is: Black American Folk Art From the Collection of Regenia Perry.* Richmond, Va.: Anderson Gallery, Virginia Commonwealth University, 1982. (Catalogue)

Rubinstein, Charlotte Streifer. *American Women Artists.* Boston: Avon Books, 1982.

Bounds, Mary C. "Art With Heart." *Dallas Morning News*, September 9, 1982.

Keasler, Jack. "Artist, 95, Once Nourished Likes of Faulkner, Steinbeck." *Jackson Daily News, Clarion Ledger*, Jackson, Miss., December 5, 1982.

Thompson, Robert F. *Flash of the Spirit*. New York: Random House, 1983.

Johnson, Jay and Ketchum, William C., Jr. *American Folk Art of the Twentieth Century*. New York: Rizzoli International Publications, 1983.

Lane, Suzette and D'Amrosio, Paul. "Folk Art in the New York State Historical Association." *Antiques*, September 1983, pp. 519–27.

Hill, Ruth Edmonds, ed. *Women of Courage—An Exhibition of Photographs by Judith Sedwick*. Cambridge, Mass.: Radcliffe College, 1984.

"Art This Week." *Minneapolis Tribune*, January 15, 1984.

Miller, Jane. "Investing." *Shreveport Times*, February 22, 1984.

Martin, Margaret. "Area Artist Celebrates Her 98th." *Shreveport Times*, March 12, 1984.

Price, Anne. "Happy 98th, Clementine." Gallery in *Sunday Magazine, Sunday Advocate*, Baton Rouge, La., March 18, 1984.

LASC Calendar, Louisiana Arts and Science Center, Baton Rouge, La., September/October/November 1984.

"Women of Courage Exhibit to Open at the New York Public Library." *Newsletter*, Schlesinger Library, Radcliffe College, Cambridge, Mass., Fall 1984.

"Gallery Lecture." Gallery in *Sunday Magazine, Sunday Advocate*, Baton Rouge, La., October 14, 1984.

American Art in Louisiana Private Collections, 1870-1970. Louisiana Arts and Science Center, Baton Rouge, La., 1985. (Catalogue)

"NOMA Exhibit to Honor Clementine Hunter's 100th." *River Parishes Guide*, Boutte, La., February 10, 1985.

"What's Doing in New Orleans." Travel Section in *New York Times*, February 17, 1985.

Kent, Joan. "Cane River Artist's Show Opens with 100th Birthday Fete." *Times Picayune*, February 24, 1985.

"Salute to Clementine." *Times Picayune*, February 24, 1985.

Ryan, Bob and Ryan, Yvonne. "Clementine Hunter: A New Orleans Salute." *Arts Quarterly*, New Orleans Museum of Art, January/February/March 1985, pp. 14–15.

"Clementine Hunter to Receive Honorary Doctorate at NSU." *Natchitoches Times*, April 11, 1985.

Read, Mimi. "Clementine Hunter." *Dixie Magazine* in *Times Picayune*, April 14, 1985.

Lamothe, Eva. "A Visit With Clementine Hunter: Painter of Visions and Dreams." *Arts Quarterly*, New Orleans Museum of Art, April/May/June 1985, pp. 32–34.

Barrett, Didi. "A Time to Reap: Late Blooming Folk Artists." *The Clarion*, Fall 1985, pp. 39–47.

Muchnic, Suzanne. "From the Cotton Fields Back Home." *Los Angeles Times*, August 14, 1986.

Stuebler, Patricia. "Art Review." *Palladium-Item*, Richmond, Ind., January 22, 1987.

Perry, Kimball. "Folk Art Speaks Up." *Journal-News*, Cincinnati, Ohio, January 26, 1987.

Jones, Anne Hudson. "The Centennial of Clementine Hunter." *Woman's Art Journal*, Spring/Summer 1987, pp. 23–27.

Lieberman, Laura. "The Southern Artist." *Southern Accents*, August 1987, pp. 106–9.

Index

Designed by Dana Bilbray and Karen Foval
Composed in Goudy Old Style by Type III.
Four-color separations by South Sea Graphic Arts.
Printed on 157 gsm Korean matte art paper on a
  Mitsubishi press and case bound with a laminated
  paper case of 135 gsm gloss art with matte lamination,
by Everbest Printing Company, Hong Kong.